FREEDOM
FROM ADDICTION 4

The Final Message

REV. WINN HENDERSON, M.D.

WORKBOOK PRESS LLC

187 E Warm Springs Rd,

Suite B285, Las Vegas, NV 89119, USA

Website: https://workbookpress.com/
Hotline: 1-888-818-4856
Email: admin@workbookpress.com

Ordering Information:

Quantity sales. Special discounts are available on quantity purchases by corporations, associations, and others.

For details, contact the publisher at the address above.

Library of Congress Control Number:

ISBN-13:   978-1-957618-71-5 (Paperback Version)

             978-1-957618-72-2 (Digital Version)

REV. DATE: 02/22/2023

Table of Contents

Forward

Are you truly happy with your life? If you can truthfully answer, "Yes," then return this book for a full refund with our congratulations!

People who get up every morning and can say, "What a wonderful day! It's great to be alive! I can't wait to get going and fulfill another piece of my destiny," are on purpose and probably don't need this book.

But what if you're not so satisfied with your life? Are you nervous or depressed? Are you lonely, fearful, or bored? Do you feel insecure, resentful, or angry? Do you think you're unappreciated or unloved? Is there an empty feeling, a void in your life? Do you suffer with feelings of guilt or shame? Do you have a lot of pain of either the physical or emotional type? Are you a worrier or a procrastinator? Do you have the idea that you'd be better off dead? Do you live life without energy and enthusiasm? Are you constantly tired? Do you need immediate gratification and pleasure with external things to feel ok?

Would it surprise you to find out that all of the feelings I just talked about are related to one problem, to one disease process? That's what I have found out in my clinical work over the last four plus decades. They are the symptoms of the disease of addiction in it's over 30 different forms.

The good news is I have also found a cure for these symptoms! If you didn't have any of the symptoms we just discussed, do you think you'd be happier, contented, and more satisfied with your life? Of course you would! A happy, successful life...that's what I want for you because that's exactly what you want for yourself. You can have it! I can absolutely guarantee you happiness, and it will come a lot faster than you think.

My first book on this subject: "The Cure of Addiction" began, quite frankly, under less than desirable circumstances in the winter of 1990. More later. It started with an unusual, revolutionary premise:

All addictive behaviors result from the same singular cause and therefore can be treated equally effectively with the same singular treatment.

In the years that have subsequently elapsed, I have had no reason to revise this belief. My clients are still being cured from the addictive disease process, and when they permanently continue the program, the cure rate is still 100%!

There have been three significant developments since the original version of this book was published. The first is a discussion of four important metaphysical questions. The correct understanding of these questions forms part of the basis for curing the disease. I have shown the reader at least one way of answering these questions which has successfully worked for a large number of clients.

Psycho-Neuro-Immunology is a branch of medicine that deals with the interrelationship between thoughts, neuro-chemicals, and the immune system. It has been amazing to me how changing one's thoughts with respect to these four questions changes in a positive way our mental and physical health, not only with respect to addictive behaviors but to many other medical conditions.

The second development represents an improvement in motivating the reader to get started and to stay committed and involved. From the beginning I had an answer that would work, but it worked only when the person was sufficiently motivated, and quite frankly most people who bought the book were not. However in the interim I have developed an auxiliary motivational program which catapults the client way past the threshold plateau.

The third development deals in developing belief or faith in the program. If you believe that this program is the inspired teaching of God, then you will be able to use the knowledge you learn here to cure your disease. I provide you with the information both from my personal life and from the Bible to support your belief.

Before we get started, I want to get something off my chest, and that is that I am not apologetic for anything I have written in this book.

The cause of this terrible disease of addiction that is ruining our country and the world is not what you have been told.

Addiction is not caused by a physical agent such as a virus, bacteria, or a protozoan. It is not a biological lack of, or an incorrect proportion of a chemical compound in the brain. It is not caused by a defective gene that has been passed down from generation to generation. It is not the result of environmental life style situations and stresses.

You have been lied to. Many addiction specialists, physicians, psychologists, social workers, ministers, and others have not told you the truth about addiction.

And what is the truth? Addiction is a spiritual illness and only a faith based treatment program can permanently cure your disease. Only in developing a strong personal spiritual relationship with God can save yourself from destruction and death.

I am a retired medical doctor and in that sense am a scientist. I believe in proving theories of disease and treatment, but I am also an ordained Christian minister who understands the spiritual connection necessary to cure this disease.

We cannot go on the way we have been going with addictive behaviors getting worse and worse every year being the direct cause of so many deaths and lives that that have been destroyed from the inside out...lives that are ruining our families and all our our other relationships.

This book is not politically correct, I'll admit, but it was not meant to be. It was meant to expose you to the truth about the most dangerous and destructive disease in the world today.

(An open letter from addiction to the world)

My name is Addiction. I am waging war against all nations and do not plan to take prisoners! Like a thief in the night, I will pillage your people, rob them of their dignity, peace of mind, and eventually their lives. The world will be in shambles before I am through.

The more the merrier: red, yellow, black, or white none are precious in my sight. Rich or poor, I have no favorites, but must admit I have fun picking on the sad and lonely, the weak and sick, and really get a kick out of young people who do not have a clue.

It is a quick seduction to entangle them in my web. They are mine from a single puff on a reefer to the pop of a rubber band and from the first taste of liquor to the bottle's last drop. It is easy to enslave them on social media screens, entice them into sexual promiscuity, and convince them that they need a cigarette or another twinkie.

There are over thirty addictive behaviors in my arsenal. Yeah, that's my greatest thrill, enslave them young and I will have them for life.

Now don't get me all wrong. I was invited to this party, and they made me the main attraction. Realizing that I was in the land of the innocent, I took advantage like a fox in a hen house. "Just try a little," I would whisper. That's all it takes, a small temptation, to get them started and they do the rest.

Making sure they have all the crappy dope and the cheap liquor they need is easy. They will snort, shoot, or drink anything. It's really fun to put pesticides and all manner of trash in their stash. It's like watching them play Russian roulette...a duel with a pistol and one bullet. They soon are mine, because there are only five empty chambers.

AIDS really adds another level of satisfaction. My ultimate thrill is to watch them struggle in pain, as their emaciated bodies lay dying. The last words they speak are often these..."What have I done to myself"?

When they are dead and gone, I get a bonus. The lives of their family is in tatters. The family is grieving because, they fiercely loved you, my prey.

The damage of addiction is vast...wide and long. Mother dies from heartache, but the real culprit was all the grief and stress that she went through. Daddy does not linger long either. Why stay when all his money was long gone before they buried you.

It does appear there is one thrill left. Your parents both go to their grave wondering if they will meet you in Heaven. They are not sure, because the last time they saw you on earth, you were blaming all your problems on them, cursing them, and demanding money.

Your Daddy always felt the bad choices he made in his life somehow rubbed off on you, and just to let you know, I did get a kick out of watching you cringe in the corner, as you watched your daddy beat your mother.

Unfortunately for me they both got right with God before they died and He rescued their sorry souls.

Most of your brothers and sisters rarely think of you today. They are just glad to be rid of the guilt, shame, and embarrassment they felt every time they looked at the shell of humanity that you ended up becoming.

Now the game is not quite finished....your little brother was closely watching all your debauchery and now he thinks he might give it a try. And surprise, surprise, that pregnancy, the baby, does not have a chance. He is just your last sacrifice.

You turned out just like I wanted...completely destroyed inside and out. Your eyes are yellow from all the booze. Hepatitis and liver damage would have killed you anyway, but it gives me great joy to announce that your appetite for momentary escape from reality took you much sooner.

A shell of your former self, alone without family, you left this world high as a kite in total oblivion to the darkness you were about to enter.....the darkness lled with all the rejected discarded souls that I have tortured and killed Your so-called friends stole your few possessions at the end and disappeared in the night before your body was cold, and 911 never got a call.

I feel like gloating. You lost your chance to make a change. All the talk of repentance and redemption went right over your head. Like sheep lead to slaughter, you were an easy target. Had you known a very simple prayer, you would not have been easy to reel in. We would never have met.

Your parents were older when they finally changed their ways, much too late to do you any good. I waited patiently until I knew you were ready. I pretended to be your friend, bolstered your low self esteem,

and made you temporarily feel like a king....but only temporarily I am proud to say.

And just a footnote to rub it in...you could have been a man or woman with everything, a nice family, a beautiful home, a pillar of the community, respected by all your family and friends. Your life could have been filled with purpose as you reached out to help your fellow man.

You could have had all this peace, joy, and happiness in life if you had opened your eyes and realized your value as a child of God. If you had allowed Him into your life to be your constant friend and adviser. God gave you all the tools you needed to complete your mission in life, but you didn't use them.

Yes, one simple prayer..."Dear God, please save me through the blood of Jesus Christ" would have protected you from me.

You know just the mention of those names: God and Jesus, completely steals all my joy. That's the reason I keep my flock constantly under my influence, so that they can not hear the sweet voice of Jesus calling them...come home, my child come home.

Yes, that is what you are...a lost child who is now out of chances. You are now lost in darkness and you are forever mine. And now, I am sure you can figure out the the story. It's been a pleasure wrecking your life and stealing your soul.

Your "friend", Addiction (aka) Satan

The thief comes only to steal and kill and destroy. I came that they may have life and have it abundantly. Addiction is merely death on the installment plan-John 10:10

How do you relate to this letter? Do you have a friend, a spouse, a child, or grandchild that you can see is suffering from the same kind of problem? Have you been frustrated that there doesn't seem to be any way to help them get rid of the problem? Are you willing to do what it takes to help them cure their disease?

The ugly truth is that you are in the middle of spiritual warfare. It is warfare between good and evil. It is a battle between God and Satan. The nature of this battle is metaphysical. It is beyond the five senses. You cannot see it, hear it, smell it, touch it, taste it, or feel it, but it is just as real as if you could.

The good news is that there is a way to help your friend, spouse, child, or grandchild. You start by helping yourself. Keep reading this book and find out how.

Chapter One - What is addiction and what is its cause?

How do we best define the terms addict or addiction? If we only think of an addict as being a homeless, penniless, friendless alcoholic or substance abuser, who being down and out is of no use to himself, or society, except as a bad example, then certainly we are not going to identify personally with the terms.

Yet over the last 80+ years since Alcoholics Anonymous' "Big Book" was published, that is exactly what many of us think. The process of denial makes it easy for us to think, "I'm not an addict. I don't need treatment." Let's not continue to define the disease in a way that makes it easy for most of us to say, "That's not me." We need a new definition of addiction, one closer to the truth.

If you have a behavior, any behavior, that is hurting you or someone you love and you can't stop it for whatever reason...then you are addicted to that behavior.

Addiction is not just the result of using drugs and alcohol. The ultimate truth of addiction is that it is not a problem of only substance abuse, but rather a problem of any number of habits gone out of control.

Addiction is an expression of our faulty way of dealing with our lack of self-esteem. Escaping addiction is more than just modifying bad habits. It means changing the nature of the relationship between us and life.

In the case of the disease of addiction, the cause is not a physical agent like a virus, bacteria, or protozoan. It is not a biological lack or incorrect proportion of a chemical compound like a neurotransmitter in the brain. It is not caused by a defective gene, and it's not the result of environmental stresses. It's none of these.

Addiction is a spiritual illness and only a treatment plan having a spiritual approach can cure the disease.

Poor self-esteem resulting from inadequate consciousness (knowing the validity of certain spiritual truths) is the underlying cause for all addictive behaviors.

Often we see an addicted individual who, on the outside, seems successful and confident in his or her life or profession. However, below the surface, on another level, he or she is actually consumed with self-doubt and lacks confidence in his or her abilities. This lack of self-esteem often develops into self-loathing or self-hate, and the individual harms himself or herself on a subconscious level by starting and continuing the unproductive maladaptive addictive behavior. The individual's feeling of powerlessness over the situation is a strong motivator in continuing the addictive cycle.

Addiction is merely a tool that Satan is using to keep you from living a happy fulfilled life. When you are not spiritually aware of the truth about your existence, your value, and the reason you are on this earth, you can be easily seduced into temporary fixes in life. These temporary fixes become less effective over time. Eventually you become a victim enslaved for life, unless you get help.

If you visualize addiction as your friend who helps you enjoy life and lets you feel like a bird on the wing without any problems, then you will most likely be one of the unfortunate individuals plagued with many problems including the possibility of a much shorter life span.

If you can visualize addiction as a robber that plans on taking everything you value in life, and wants to totally destroy and kill you, then you might have a chance.

Chapter Two - Concerning your desire to help the people you love

Many books have already been written speak to individuals (if and when they get ready to make a change in their life). Most people reading this book will not only be an addict themselves, but also the person in the the life of the person that they care about who wants to bring about a change and cessation of addiction.

You recognize and realize that your spouse, child, grandchild, or others that you love are ruining their lives by their addictive behaviors. You want to help, but you don't know how. You want to take an active role in helping to cure the disease of addiction in the people you love. You want to know how you can make this goal your mission or at least a part of your mission in life.

The bible gives us instruction on how to raise a child: "Train up a child in the way he should go; even when he is old he will not depart from it." Proverbs 22:6. The way you train a child is through your example. "Scripture is breathed out by God and is profitable for teaching, for reproof, for correction, and for training in righteousness that the man of God may be competent, equipped for every good work." 2 Timothy 3:16-17

The parent is the role model for the child or in some cases the grandchild. Either you have been a good role model or a bad role model. Either you have modeled addictive behavior or you have modeled freedom from addiction. You know all the good and bad influences you have made in your child's life.

I will throw in a variable that may give rise to parents and grandparents. It takes at least 7 praises to counterbalance just one criticism, and criticism lowers self-esteem. The lack of positive feedback for the good things the child does may lead the child to do negative things because he or she gains attention by doing so.

Proactive parents provide an environment of love and safety, serve as a good role models, and take an active part and interest in all facets of their child's life.

Parents tend to raise their children the way they themselves were raised. If you were a product of good or bad parenting, your parenting skills are primarily based on the model your parents set.

Generations are dominated by role model parenting skills. Addictive behaviors are sometimes generational. If the parent smokes, uses drugs, abuses alcohol, or overeats for example, the child has to live in that environment. Like a sponge the child soaks it in and they start believing that this way of life is the way that they should be living. It is likely that they will repeat the same behavior(s) in their own life. In order for your children to have the best lives they possibly could have, it is your responsibility as a parent to show them the potential of an addictive free life.

I have used parents as the example here, but addiction is everybody's problem (parents, children, siblings, grand parents, friends, neighbors, business associates, the community, and the world).

Addiction is affecting all their lives, lives that are touched with stress related physical and psychological problems. Financial considerations are also part of this dialogue. The individual's financial woes often create financial burdens on family and friends.

It also touches their employer's bottom line. As absenteeism from work increases productivity decreases.

Addictions play a major part in rising crime rates in the community.

Regardless of your relationship to the addicted individual, you should first examine yourself to make sure you are going to be a good role model and a positive influence in the individual's life.

Medical missionary Dr. Albert Schweitzer said, "I don't know what your destiny will be, but one thing I know: The only ones among you who will be really happy are those who have sought and found how to serve." Romans 12:2 reads: "Do not be conformed to this world, but be transformed by the renewal of your mind, that by testing you may discern what is the will of God, what is good and acceptable and perfect."

This book will teach you that we all have a space in our lives that is filled with either healthy, positive things or filled with unhealthy negative things. The positive contents that fill the space bring all the ingredients that promote happiness and a sense of worth (high self-esteem). The negative contents seem to temporarily fill the space, but repeating the addictive cycle creates a habit that is doomed to eventually hurt not only yourself, but also the people in your life that you care about.

Let's use overeating as an example. Overeating is a major underlining cause of health problems in this country. If not addressed, the addictive behavior of overeating will negatively touch both the physical and mental health of the individual. As the weight increases, the downward spiral of self-esteem makes the addiction worse. The bottom line results are general health problems, mental problems, loss of productivity, and a compromise of the life span of the individual. You may consider some addictions worse than others, but they all present problems that lead the individual down the rabbit hole of an unhealthy life.

Some addictions such as smoking are socially tolerated, but lives are adversely changed. The desire to smoke limits quality time in relationships, contributes to financial woes, and shortens the life span.

Any harmful behavior that an individual cannot stop doing is an addiction. Even watching too much late night TV causes sleep deprivation that over time will cause health problems. It is time that individuals stop casting stones at other people's addictions, because more than likely they have a behavior that they themselves cannot stop doing. All these behaviors are caused or invited into lives because individuals do not appreciate their personal value. We are all children of God and as such we share a heavenly Father. He cares for each of us equally and wants only the best for us.

Circumstances in our lives may redirect our focus. We lose sight of our value as a child of God, even to the point that we become destructive to ourselves. This behavior has far-reaching influence in how our life unfolds. It is only through reconnecting with God, that we return to a place where our identity means something of value to us. Jesus, the Son of God, paved the way for our reconnection with God. He died on the cross to enable us to have access to God.

My goal with this book is to provide tools and a helping hand to you and the person in your life you are concerned about. Reconnecting with God is the end result. Once reconnected individuals feel completely different about themselves. They finally get it...the reason they were born, why they are here, what they need to be doing with their life, and where they are going when their life is complete. When they get it, there is no way that they would want to do things that are harmful to their bodies or shorten their life span. Their lives will be redirected to seek out the knowledge and resources they need to start, maintain, and complete the mission they know they were born to do.

How do near death experiences relate to curing addictions? There may be controversy on the validity of such experiences, but the millions of people who share this experience walked away with a new life perspective. They felt a dramatic change and desire to do their part to make the world a better place. Negative feelings changed into positive feelings. They developed a sense of gratitude for what they have. They now understood the truly important things in life. They realized and embraced the mission they had been given.

However not all the near-death experiences are good ones. The bad ones are very dramatic, because they experience a nightmarish situation. In these situations the mere mention of Jesus or God have kept the demons at bay. Asking to be saved was the ultimate request that rescued them. They were shown the good and bad sides of their life experience. Good or bad, the end result of near death experiences is a life changing event. Forever changed, they desired to be a positive influence in the lives of their family, their community, and in the world.

Your mission large or small has to do with bringing this message of addiction and subsequent treatment and cure (through your example) to someone else. You will become the co-object of the treatment and cure of this disease. By doing so you can help yourself and the people you love and the whole world in the process. You first have to educate yourself and be able to address any addictive behavior that you have. At that point you will be better able to help others by teaching them what you have learned. More than likely you have a behavior that you cannot stop even though you know it is hurting you or someone you love. Until you cure your own addictive behavior(s), you will not be able to help anyone else. Your addiction may not have an equal social stigma that your loved one suffers from, but it is an addiction nonetheless which stems from the same cause.

Apples, oranges, and bananas are all fruits, just as smoking, drugs, over-eating, or any number of behaviors are all addictions. You cannot continue your own addiction and be the example you need to be to help someone else. This book was written to teach you how to cure yourself from your addiction(s) and in turn then you by example will be able to help the person you are concerned about.

Chapter Three - Will My Ashes Speak My Truth?

It's time for your grand finale. Your time on earth has come to an end. There is no time left to make corrections or to make amends. Your friends are all gathered in a peaceful chapel listening to soft music. They are congregated to honor your life and accomplishments.

Each in his own way absorbs the enormity of the situation knowing that this is a day that they too will face in the not so distant future. Their futures loom closer as the understanding of death becomes momentarily the focus of their attention.

If you could reach out in love and embrace these wonderful people what would you want them to remember about your life? Has your life been one that can serve as a beacon that they can emulate? Did you fully realize your aspirations and dreams without being led astray by the distractions of the world? What advice would you give this captive audience? Would you share your ups and downs, your achievements and failures? Would your formula for meeting life's challenges serve as a worthy road map for them?

Take the time right now to visualize your funeral. Pretend that you were able to speak to them and give a final testimony of your life. Have the people you have touched in your life come away from the experience better for having known you? Have you used your God-given talents for the betterment of mankind or have you hidden them unused to be tucked away in your casket with a body that is now discarded after years of use and abuse? If any of these scenarios fit your life it is time to make changes now.

If you wait until that final day then you've waited too long. You cannot rewrite the story of your life nor paint new scenes from your past. Reality is the life you have lived. The world was waiting for your impact and watching as your life unfolded. You can not leave beautiful memories if you don't take the time now to decide what you really want out of life. Make your life count for something. Let it serve mankind.

If you use the life of Jesus as your example you will be long remembered for your contribution and loving presence on the earth. Start now by setting the building blocks for a compelling vision, a personal mission for your life.

Jesus is the example God gave us and it will serve mankind well if you strive to do your very best to emulate Him. Each day is a new chapter in your legacy that you will leave behind. God and the world is watching.

Chapter Four - Overview

There are many types of addictive behaviors and they fall into one of the following groups: Pornography, Racism, Gossiping, Co-Dependency (Control), Substance Abuse (Marijuana- Alcohol- Hallucinogens- Opiates- Inhalants- Depressants- Stimulants- Anabolic Steroids), Gambling, Kleptomania (Shoplifting), Smoking (Nicotine), Sociopathic (narcissistic) Behavior, Over or Under Eating, Sexual/Non-Sexual Abuse, Workaholism, Excitement, Power/ Greed, Teenage Rebellion, Sexual Compulsions, Overspending, Negative Thinking, TV/Computer/Gaming/Smart Phone overuse, and Hoarding/Colectaholism.

A self-perpetuating addictive cycle is formed which starts with the basic underlying cause of the disease...low self-esteem. Low self-esteem directly results from an insufficiently developed consciousness (the level of understanding of four important spiritual questions of life to be discussed later). People with low self-esteem develop feelings and emotions like: loneliness, unhappiness, discontentment, emotional pain, anxiety, emptiness, depression, "a void", unworthiness, lack of love, lack of acceptance, unsuccessfulness, sorrow, fear, insecurity, sadness, boredom, resentment, self-pity, a desire for immediate gratification and pleasure, and suicidal thoughts.

The individual wants relief from these symptoms and proceeds to treat himself or herself with what is most common and available...the addictive behaviors. In fact these addictive behaviors do work to some extent to increase feelings of self worth, but only temporarily, (as long as the behavior is being used). The trouble with this solution to the problem is that every addictive behavior has side effects and complications that are bad for you, and you can't stay drunk or high forever. When the side effects and complications hit you, your self - esteem decreases and you use the behavior again. It is a vicious cycle.

Death ultimately interrupts the cycle, and often prematurely, but in the meantime, the individual suffers all kinds of losses like...money, possessions, personal freedom, family relationships, physical disabilities, and others. As a result of these losses, bad feelings (self-pity, doubt, insecurity, guilt, anger, shame, fear, and others) develop. These negative emotions increase and reinforce low self-esteem. The addictive cycle is now formed, and it continues to turn until it is broken.

Understanding the problem in this way explains why trying to treat the end result of the disease process ...the addictive behaviors...has been relatively unsuccessful. Individual self will alone is just not strong enough to stop an addictive process. ***Addiction is stronger***. If one is able to resist a particular behavior, and this can be done for a finite period of time, the problem resurfaces later or the addictive behavior is changed and expresses itself in another form.

In order to be permanently effective, treatment must be directed at the cause of the problem...low self-esteem and insufficient spiritual

consciousness. When one corrects the cause, there is no longer a need nor desire for the addictive behavior.

Now, most people want balance in their lives, because when balanced, life is manageable. A balanced life reinforces a good self image, sustains the ability to be able to love one's self and others, and helps the understanding of how to best use and retain the assets one has earned. It is important to to have enough spirituality in one's life to keep it from being unmanageable and ripe for self-destruction.

Note that religion and spirituality are not the same thing. Religion has more to do with doctrine and dogma whereas spirituality has more to do with understanding the metaphysical truths that often lay outside of one's five senses.

To treat addictive illnesses, one must do something to improve self-esteem and spiritual consciousness. My program deals with five treatment steps which do exactly that.

The five treatment steps are:

Continuing education.
Becoming more physically fit.
Becoming more creative.
Helping others and forgiving them.
Developing spiritually.

Fortunately, when the treatment plan is followed, and the individual truly wants the plan to work and believes it will work, now, for the first time, there is an available recovery program which can be effective in every case where true desire and belief is present.

The treatment plan uses an easy to follow "Cook Book" approach with a motivational daily treatment calendar that anyone can use effectively.

The most important part of this plan is developing one's spirituality, and this can be accomplished by: Affirmations, Prayer and Meditation, The 12 Step Program (revised), Changing Associations, Organized Religion, Bible study, or Inspirational Reading.

Together the five treatment steps fit into a cohesive package. Validation of this treatment is simple. It works!

Chapter Five - Why do we have addictive problems anyway?

Would it not have been simpler for our creator to make a world where people just enjoyed everything but never became addicted or out of control?

If the Garden of Eden experience had worked out better we would not need to answer this question. However you know how it did work out and so here is the answer.

The answer is yes, it would have been simpler, but addictive behavior sooner or later causes suffering and pain, misery, and losses. Sooner or later, if the addictive behaviors don't kill you, they hurt you bad enough that you seek relief from the suffering. It is precisely this pain, and the subsequent chance to learn and grow from it that required the creation of the process of addiction in the first place. In this light, addiction can be seen, not as a drug or alcohol problem, nor a gambling problem, nor a relationship problem and not as a problem only of a few unfortunate individuals, but as a problem for all of us.

You may have bought this book because you wanted to help someone you love escape from the terrible disease of addiction and you did not know how to help them. Most all of the 7.9 billion people on the planet are addicted to something.

First, let's find out if you are one of them. Read the list of psychological symptoms that are symptoms of the disease of addiction. Do you suffer from one or more of these symptoms... anxiety, depression, loneliness, unhappiness, discontentment, emotional pain, emptiness, "a void", unworthiness, lack of love, lack of acceptance, unsuccessfulness, sorrow, fear, insecurity, sadness, boredom, resentment, self-pity, a desire for immediate gratification and pleasure, or suicidal thoughts?

Now read the descriptions of the various addictive behaviors [Chapter 14]. Do you have one of these behaviors and is it hurting you or someone you love? If you suffer from one or more of the symptoms of the disease and have a behavior that you can't quit which is hurting you or someone you love, then you suffer from the disease of addiction.

In your life do you have someone: a spouse, a child, a grandchild, or some other person that you love very much who also suffers from this disease and you want to help?

There are only two things that you can do to help. **The first is to cure yourself from the disease so that you can be a good role model and mentor to the person you want to help**. [Everything that you need to accomplish this is written in this book].

Once you have cured yourself from this disease, show your loved one what it has done in your life and how you are different now. **Begin a prayer campaign and ask God to use this change to convict your love one of his or hers need to do the same thing.** God is faithful to his promises. He will answer your prayer.

"There hath been no temptation overtaken you but such as is common to mankind: but God is faithful. He will not let you be tempted beyond what you can bear. But when you are tempted, he will also provide a way out so that you can endure it." 1 Corinthians 10:13

Chapter Six - Addiction and Balance

One can burn, yearn for extremes

But balance in life

Is often the means

To richness in life.

Or that's what it seems to me.

The balance scale remembers well

Our thoughts and actions done.

At the end of time

We hope to find

At last our battle's won.

Life need not be unmanageable,

Really that is true.

We hardly need more problems

To help us muddle through.

Yet life has a habit

Of dealing us our hand

So things often turn out,

Not as though we'd planned.

And balance in life

Is just like you thought.

The extremes of your judgment

Portend what you wrought.

The balance beam swings quite wildly

when you're out of control.

First this way, then that way,

It soon takes its toll

On living or dying,

And the fate of your soul.

Productivity, creativity,

self-love, and the rest...

Balance in life

is the means to success.

Freedom From Addiction 4

It may not seem dashing,

Exciting, or fun,

But balance is steady

as the race it is run.

Now addiction is cunning.

It's a disease of extremes.

And balance more narrow,

You know what that means.

That balance is needed

to straighten your course.

That balance can shield you

from external remorse.

That balance will guide you

toward your journey's end.

That balance will save you,

will save you, my friend!

Chapter Seven - A Disease With A Spiritual Cause

There's something missing in the search for happiness and fulfillment in our lives which is mistakenly sought through food, alcohol, drugs, sex, and all the other addictive behaviors. We try to find the answer to that missing something in things that are common and available.

Imagine Libra's scale with physical pleasures and pursuits in the form of eggs in one basket and spiritual eggs in the other. Pretend there are only so many eggs available for an individual's baskets. When a physical trait is removed, the egg moves to the spiritual side, and vice versa. To load up on one side of the scale lightens the other side.

Now visualize the physical basket loaded with delights of the five senses: taste, touch, smell, sight, hearing. Visualize the spiritual basket filled with spiritual traits: love, contentment, acceptance, joy, security, compassion, courage, patience, happiness, and peace-of-mind.

Yielding to addictive behaviors involves loading your eggs in the physical basket and taking them away from the spiritual side. As more eggs are transferred from the spiritual basket to the physical basket, one's life becomes less balanced and less manageable. With a relative spiritual void, a subconscious aching need develops. To succeed in filling this void, eggs must be transferred back from the physical basket. As spiritual efforts increase, physical symptoms decrease.

So how do we fill this spiritual void? We can accomplish this by following a spiritual path in our journey through life. Some examples are 12 step programs, church attendance, Bible study, prayer, meditation, and detaching from materialistic possessions and associations.

Which spiritual path works the best for you? This question is best answered through prayer and meditation. One asks for advice and waits on the answer until it comes.

Everyone's degree of difficulty and distress from the symptoms of addiction are different, and one individual's symptoms never exactly equals another. Fortunately the type and degree make absolutely no difference in the treatment program, which is the same for all.

This book will provide you the understanding needed for spiritual growth. You may not be ready today to admit your helplessness and to surrender control back to God, but hopefully this exposure will give you the answers you need when you are ready.

Look deep inside yourself. What is your life trying to tell you? When you are ready there will be someone to help you. Have faith because faith is what it takes to succeed, to walk away from your pain and suffering.

Chapter Eight - I'm special

In all the world there is nobody like me. Since the beginning of time, there has never been another person exactly like me. Nobody has my smile. Nobody has my eyes, my nose, my hair, my hands, my voice. I'm special. No one has my handwriting. Nobody anywhere has my tastes for food or music or art. No one sees things just as I do. In all of time, there's been no one who laughs like me, no one who cries like me, and what makes me laugh and cry will never provoke identical laughter and tears from anybody else, ever. No one reacts to any situation just as I would react. I'm special. I'm the only one in all of creation who has my unique set of abilities. Oh, there will always be somebody who is better at one of the things that l am good at, but no one in the universe can reach the quality of my combination of talents, ideas, abilities, and feelings. Like a roomful of musical instruments, some may excel alone, but none can match the symphonic sound when they are all played together. I'm special. Through all of eternity no one will ever look, talk, walk, think, or do things like me. I'm special. I'm rare. And in all rarity there is great value. Because of my rare value, I need not attempt to imitate others. I will accept, yes celebrate my differences. I'm special, and I'm beginning to realize it's no accident that I'm special. I'm beginning to see that God made me special for a very special purpose. He must have a job for me that no one else can do

Out of all the billions of applicants, only one is qualified, only one has the right combination of what it takes. That one is me because...I'm special!

Chapter Nine - 17 rules to live by

These 17 rules come from my now deceased friend, Og Mandino's book, *A Better Way to Live.* I have altered them slightly for you to use as affirmations. Og gave a speech decades ago in Dallas Texas. He received the longest standing ovation that I have ever heard given to anyone at any time.

I count my blessings.

Today, and everyday, I deliver more than I am getting paid to deliver.

Whenever I make a mistake or get knocked down by life, I don't look back at it too long. I shake off my blunders.

I always reward my long hours of labor and toil in the very best way, surrounded by my family.

I build this day on a foundation of pleasant thoughts. I am a creature of God, and have the power to achieve any dream by lifting up my thoughts.

I let my actions speak for me, but I am forever on guard against the terrible traps of false pride and conceit that can halt my progress.

Each day is a special gift from God, and while life may not always be fair, I never allow the pains, hurdles, and handicaps of the moment to poison my attitude and plans for myself and my future.

I never again clutter my days and nights with so many menial and unimportant things that I have no time to accept a real challenge when it comes along.

I live this day as if it will be my last.

Beginning today, I treat everyone I meet, friend or foe, loved one or stranger, as if they were going to be dead at midnight.

I laugh at myself and at life.

I never neglect the little things.

I welcome every morning with a smile. I look on the new day as another special gift from my creator, another golden opportunity to complete what I was unable to finish yesterday.

I will achieve my grand dream, a day at a time, so I set my goals for each day.

I never allow anyone to rain on my parade and thus cast a pall of gloom and defeat on the entire day. Nothing external can have any power over me unless I permit it.

I search for the seed of good in every adversity.

I realize true happiness lies within me.

Wise men, since the beginning of time, have been telling us that all we achieve, or fail to achieve, results from how we think. James Allen told us that good thoughts bear good fruit. Roman Marcus Aurelius told us that our life is what our thoughts make it. Norman Vincent Peale once remarked, "As he thinketh in his heart, so is he." Buddha said, "All that we are is the result of what we have thought. The mind is everything. What we think, we become." And Jesus said, "What things so ever ye desire, when ye pray, believe that ye receive them, and ye shall have them."

And so it is. If you will but believe in the tremendous power of positive affirmation and act on that belief, you can have anything or accomplish anything not contradictory to the laws of God or society.

Chapter Ten The Secret to Success

There is nothing in life that needs to be feared,

Only understood.

There's nothing in life that can't be achieved,

If its cause is good.

If you have a goal in life, set your course

And then stay with it.

No matter what happens, don't give up

And never, never quit it.

When the best of things are not in reach,

Hitch your dreams upon a star.

And then until your dreams come true,

Make the best of things that are.

The secret to success, my friend

As you walk down life's long trail,

You'll never be defeated

If you act like you can't fail.

Chapter Eleven The Four Questions

This is the exciting part! If you have never contemplated the four most important spiritual questions in life nor sought the answers, no wonder your self-esteem is not high enough to save you from the effects of the disease of addiction.

There are two equally valid ways of discovering new knowledge. One way is observation and the other is contemplation. An example of observation was Newton's discovery of gravity by watching an apple fall. An example of contemplation was Einstein's discovery of the concept $E=MC^2$.

The four questions discussed in this chapter and their answers came to me during a time of prayer and meditation through contemplation.

Contemplation

On what plane of existence

Does perfect knowledge now exist?

And where does supraconsciousness reside?

Truth, light, and understanding live

In the attic of one's mind.

And mind is the builder

Of all things large and small.

Contemplation is the method

To reach one's port-of-call.

Throughout all time, discovery,

Came most by tapping in

To the pool of wisdom that

Connects beginning and end.

Newton had his theories.

Galileo's world was round.

Di Vinci dreamed of flying machines.

Mendel's peas sprung from the ground.

Einstein contemplated space, mass, relativity.

All the world's great thinkers

Thought thoughts they couldn't see.

The answer to every question

Has always existed my friend.

The question that needs the answer is....

How do we tap in?

Remember the scenario of the addiction disease process? Initially our consciousness had not been expanded sufficiently due to our failure to deal with and understand the four questions. As a result we had less than an adequate sense of our own value or self-worth. We tried to fix this negative feeling with what was common and available...the addictive behaviors. The addictive behaviors, and the basic disease process itself, caused symptoms like anxiety, depression, loneliness, fear, boredom, emptiness, pain, guilt, unhappiness, resentment, lack of energy, and the need for immediate gratification and pleasure.

Between the bad side effects and complications of the addictive behaviors, and secondary effects of the symptoms, self-esteem was further damaged and the addictive cycle established. To cure the disease, all that is necessary is to break the cycle. This is done by increasing self-esteem, and the fastest and easiest way to do this is to understand the answers to the four questions.

Question #1- Who Am I?

Humans have a dual heritage. We have an earthly physical component and a spiritual component. We see the earthly component and accept and believe in it. No problem there. We can't see the spiritual part, since it is beyond our five senses, so we have problems accepting this part of our being and in believing that we are spiritual creatures also.

You won't get very far in this healing program if you can't accept this understanding. It is critical to your self-esteem and here's why.

You know how the physical side works. The father contributes half of the genetic information necessary to form your first cell and the mother contributes the other half. From this first cell, every other cell in your body is formed. Therefore you are actually part of your parents and have their characteristics.

Now the spiritual side works the same way. Your spiritual creator is God, and since God is your spiritual Father, you have in that part of your heritage His characteristics. This part of you is perfect, because your spiritual Father is perfect. Remember that most people refer to Jesus as Jesus Christ and that dual name implies a dual heritage, Jesus from the physical side and Christ from the spiritual side.

Now tell me, if you really believe what I have just told you, and you answered the question this way: I am a child of God, how would you see yourself and your self-worth? Knowing that part of you is perfect, could you think of yourself as worthless or not good enough anymore? How could you, knowing this truth, continue to hurt and mistreat such a valuable treasure? Would this information cause you to be kinder to yourself and love yourself more?

At this point, some of the readers are going to say, "I'm not convinced. That's just your opinion." I could make any number of arguments to support my case, but let me give you two to consider.

In the first place, for those of you who embrace the Christian faith, Jesus, the founder of that religion, once said in front of a group of ordinary people when teaching them how to pray, "Our Father." Remember the beginning of The Lord's Prayer? He didn't say, "My Father," which would have made a distinction between Him and all the others to whom he was speaking. He said, "Our Father," which should reasonably indicate that Jesus believed we had the same spiritual father. Obviously He was not referring to His earthly father. Jesus believed He was the spiritual son of God and that all the people He was addressing were also the spiritual sons and daughters of God.

The second point I would like to make is that this is a practical belief. With this belief, you will be able to generate enough self-esteem to stop your suffering and cure the disease. Without it, you probably won't.

Later I will explain affirmations and how to use them to quickly change the way you think about things. Your affirmation to accomplish this part of the program is....I am a child of God.

Question #2- Where Did I Come From?

The second question implies something different than "Baptist Hospital". The significant answer deals with one's spiritual origin. The question is a continuation and development of the first question. Obviously if one has trouble accepting the first question, then there will be a lot of confusion about the second one.

If you accept the premise that you are a child of God, then it is reasonable to believe that you came from God initially. We could get into a philosophical discussion of religion, but that is not absolutely necessary to understand the importance of developing one's self-esteem by the proper answer to this question. If you are God's child, then your problems are His problems. Of course He's much better at fighting your battles and solving your problems than you will ever be. Most clients who are successful with this program answer the question by affirming, "I came from God."

Question #3- What Am I Doing Here?

This is the question that most of us have not yet significantly considered nor tried to answer in a meaningful way. Still, each of us has a purpose or destiny to justify our creation.

Can you see that if you had a destiny, something that you felt to be very worthwhile and something you knew you must accomplish before you died, that your priorities would be different? You'd look at your relationship to other people differently. You'd have a different way of looking at yourself, and you'd have a vested interest in protecting yourself from harm lest you were not able to accomplish your purpose. Having a purpose dramatically increases one's self-esteem. And this is why it is absolutely necessary to satisfactorily answer this question.

For many of us, the answer is that my purpose is to go to a job so that I can make enough money on which to live. This is not good enough because this is not a highly self-esteeming answer. Alternatively few people would argue with the concept that service to others is a very worthwhile endeavor in life. Service to others is a life purpose that increases self-esteem.

We all can accomplish service to others, but we don't all do it the same way. Each of us have different talents, different interests, different needs, and different concerns. It is our individual responsibility to find the answer to this question and then to act on it. **It doesn't matter as much what you believe your destiny to be as long as you have a destiny to believe in.**

Here's the question to ask yourself. **If I didn't have to worry about what anybody thought, not my parents, not my wife or husband, not my children, and not society in general, and if I had no limitations, neither financial, educational, nor of any other kind, what would I want to accomplish in this life that would make me the happiest, the most contented, and best justify my existence?**

Now repeat this affirmation: **"God, I'm ready to learn my true destiny. Give me a burning desire for something to accomplish with my life."** Simply ask the question, continually repeat the affirmation, and wait on the answer. It will come. Meditation will speed up the process.

The other part of the answer to this question, and it is interconnected to what we just discussed, is that we are here, much as being in school, to learn lessons and grow and develop spiritually. We often accomplish significant progress toward this goal by service to others.

The fathering of one's true heart's desire may change the whole universe. Whatever your heart's burning desire turns out to be is ok. That's your correct destiny. But destinies can change and they do. If sometime in the future you feel your purpose in life has changed, fine. Go with your new purpose. One thing you can absolutely count on in life is that things change.

Your affirmation here could be, "I am here to do God's will in my life, and thereby fulfill my destiny."

Question #4 Where Am I Going When I'm Done?

Fear, and fear of death in particular, is one of the most universal characteristics found in people who suffer from addictive behaviors. Fear of death, depending on the survey, is the first or second greatest fear we have. Fear in general seems to stop spiritual development dead in it's tracks.

Actually there are only three commonly held beliefs about death and none of them need to be particularly terrifying. The first belief is that when we die we merely cease to exist. The electricity is turned off. The lights go out. No after life, nothing. You just cease to exist. If this is the case, we can be sorry that we didn't live longer, but there is no reason to be afraid of this scenario.

The second belief is that there is a "heaven" and a "hell" and that we go to one or the other depending on how we lived our lives and what we believed religiously. If one believes in this scenario, one merely has to do what is prescribed by the religious teachings he or she has been taught and then one automatically goes to "heaven." This too is not frightening.

The third commonly held belief is that the soul cannot be destroyed and continues on forever whether it is in a physical body or not. Reincarnation is the name of the plan that allows the soul to re-inhabit another physical form at a later time with the object of continued spiritual growth. In this view, death is merely a temporary transition from one state to another.

If one understands that there is really nothing to fear in death, one can live more fully and can focus on the essence of life and in accomplishing one's destiny. Ridding oneself of this fear empowers the individual and increases his or her self-esteem.

Death Be Not Feared

When life deals misfortune,

Be it terribly cruel,

Have the strength to continue

Like thread on a spool.

Whatever your trouble,

Of whatever kind,

Have courage and faith

Face your danger in time.

If doubt seems to plague you,

It's good for your health,

Share your courage with others.

Keep your fear to yourself.

Cause it's not what you've lost

But what you have left.

The fear of surviving

Should not end in death.

For fear of the unknown

Plays tricks on your mind.

First this way, then that way,

No comfort you find.

And not knowing the future

Is unnerving at best.

But not bowing to fear

Is the ultimate test.

Have courage on ending.

Death be not feared.

Remember with pleasure

The course that you've steered.

And remember that death

Is not dark and cold.

It's merely the carriage

To transport your soul

To the next step in living.

To peace, truth, and light.

Your developing spirit

Can sense that it's right.

And as you pass over

Don't be afraid.

For in ending one cycle,

Another is made.

Now give up your body

If it's day is done,

And exchange it for spirit.

Your victory is won!

Your affirmation for question four could be answered as...When I'm done, I will return to God.

Chapter Twelve Motivation

"*If you always do what you have always done, you will always get what you have always got!*" Anonymous

The purpose of this chapter is simply my attempt to accelerate and enhance the motivational process to a level where you have no choice but to recognize the real possibility of future happiness in your life and to make a commitment to attain that goal. I want to provide the necessary counsel to help you get to the point in your life where you can articulate and put into motion the innovative principles outlined in this book.

It is my hope that you will be drawn to understand and be inspired by this emerging vision as you make a commitment and allow it to unfold in your life, making you the best that you can be. Everything about you and the way you live your life will mirror the conscious way you understand and shape your "vision" of life. New pathways will open as you begin to make choices to replace negative feelings with positive ones. You will in turn experience all the positive effects of the changes taking place in your life. This new found creative process can increase your internal spiritual energy, creating the opportunity for growth, but whether or not you actually make changes will ultimately be a choice with which you will have to come to terms.

I have learned that until a person really desires to do what's best for him or her, no philosophy, no education, nor any law can force the individual to change.

Spiritual and physical balance and harmony are essential for the successful completion of everything we attempt, and through prayer and meditation we can experience the growing spiritual and physical levels of attunement as our mind and body merge together.

You will gradually develop the self-discipline necessary to control the ego as it fights for position in your life. When the self-centered ego finally loses ground to the creator's spiritual power, you will begin to experience inner peace and harmony that will assist you with the sometimes difficult steps necessary to change and gain control over your basic nature. If you remain steadfast and receptive to this inner spiritual guidance, you will develop a strong desire to help others and you will automatically find ways to share your blessings.

This constant focus on self-improvement will serve as inspiration to even greater growth. However as you learn to sort out your own personal values and attitudes toward life, don't be too hard on yourself if you are a little less than perfect. Remember to forgive yourself, and always try to accept and learn new lessons along the way. You may find yourself embroiled in a conscious internal revolution as your reality or truth becomes more and more positive.

Defense mechanisms from the past may rear their ugly heads to further distort your perception of the truth, but you will eventually learn to let go and to understand how these behaviors are bad for you. Before long these negative defense mechanisms are where they belong...in your past.

Your new choices will allow you to look at everything in a new way. You will need to start examining all your old habits to see if they fit in your life. If they do not belong, replace them with more positive behaviors. Make up your own personal set of affirmations that serve as reminders to keep you on target to more enhanced awareness and more intelligent and appropriate responses.

It will be necessary for you to interrupt your current thought patterns. Changing the way you think about things is necessary to achieve a complete transformation of your state of mind, beliefs, and values.

Learn to associate pain to your past bad behaviors and pleasure to your new behaviors or patterns. Pain and negative emotions go hand in hand to get us ready to change. By including these emotional elements in your thoughts, you set something powerful into motion, and your chance of success increases. Each accomplishment with a favorable outcome will make you stronger in your resolve.

Strive to avoid habitual negative rituals in favor of more pleasant ones of pleasure and positivism. In the work of stitching a quilt, a teacher is often needed to produce the high quality pattern that will ultimately increase the quilt's value. The same is true of life.

The use of role models will permit you to anchor to patterns that have already produced desirable results in another's life. Always choose someone who reflects the things you want in your life. If you surround yourself with people you respect and want to model, you will find that these very same people will provide the most help in fulfilling your destiny or life's work.

Learn to welcome change when something you are doing does not work. Keep in your mind what you wish to accomplish, and what is the overall pattern you wish to weave into your future.

Relax so you can enjoy the peak experiences you identify with on your journey to self-realization. Be receptive to making changes in your rules or value system as you learn to embrace a more workable philosophy.

Remember, nothing will ever be accomplished if you fail to condition yourself for success. Set your goals and start immediately to put them into place. Decide how you want your life to be, and then take action to make it a reality. Are you happy with the way your life is right now? If you continue the way you are, will the good things outweigh the bad?

A good way to start would most definitely include taking inventory. List all the bad things that could and probably will happen if you do not change things. Now shift gears, and list all the good things that are possible or could conceivably happen in your life if you make a commitment to make the changes that I have been encouraging.

Stretch your imagination. Let the sky be the limit. Be honest in your evaluation and take your personal desires into consideration. By the time this exercise is finished, you should have a significant desire to implement a change in the direction in which your life is going.

If you do not accept the challenge to move forward, this book will be of little value to you. If you do your very best to follow the program laid out in this book, I guarantee you will find your future full of promise, peace, and happiness.

Unfortunately, sometimes we are not ready to graduate from "the school of our mistakes," but we can make positive strides in our lives if we learn from them and forge ahead confidently making the corrections needed to insure a better future. The very way you define life can serve as your formula for future happiness. Be creative, purify your thought processes, remain constant in your visualization of happiness, and always follow your personal internal guidance system. Evaluate your progress periodically to keep on course.

Ask yourself questions designed to keep you truthful in your assessment: What do I want my life to be like in 5, 10, or 20 years from now? What legacy would I like to leave behind? **At best, life is short, so stop procrastinating.** Set your goals and begin now to make your dreams come true. Daydreaming should become a part of the past, replaced by hands on participation. This personal investment in the development of both physical and spiritual patterns will keep you focused on your mission in life.

Once you realize how valuable a person you are, you will understand that you deserve to have your desires fulfilled. There are no duplicates of you. Like a potter at work, your creator made you distinctive and different from every other person on earth. You are a precious, and very valuable work of art that possesses God's love and spirit within your being.

Wake up! Realize who you are. Put the spotlight on your life. Play up your good points and use all the talents you have at your disposal. Accept yourself and learn to love and appreciate your individuality. Place value on your life as you explore your weaknesses, and learn the methods that will facilitate the changes you are seeking to put into place in your life.

It pays to glance at your watch every once in a while to remind yourself that time belongs to no man. Your time here on earth is limited, so make the most of it. Recognize and start fulfilling your destiny. You were not put here to waste the potential of your creator's masterpiece. He gave you everything you need to succeed. Without exception, a special particular mission belongs to you and you alone.

We were born with infinite possibilities for greatness, but you will get more breaks in life if you are willing to make needed changes in your way of thinking. Change is a concept you have to embrace if you are to maximize your contribution to the world. Recognize what a wonderful human being you are with many valuable potential contributions to the world. Every happy and content individual has at some time experienced the same spiritual awakening that you are embracing now. By inviting the presence of God into your life, you merely give up the driver's seat. Simply ask and you will receive divine direction that will point you to the pathway you need to be on in order to accomplish your mission here on earth.

Many people squander their talents and possibilities of greatness by means of escapism, making no contribution that could justify their existence on this planet. Time is limited. We do not get to stay forever. Psychologically sometimes we deny this fact, but in our hearts we know it's true.

Since I use every resource at my disposal to reach as many people as possible, I must try another idea on you. If you are not motivated enough to work the program for your own benefit, maybe you would reconsider if you realized how much it would help the important people in your life. If you have children, they will undoubtedly be in the position to benefit from your commitment to change the way you think about things.

I would like to share with you some of the things that are very important in your child's life. Hopefully as I show you the ways you can influence your child, you will more readily embrace a lifestyle change for yourself. As a parent, you have an impact in the world simply by being a mother or a father living together in healthy, peaceful harmony. A child's sense of security is established very early in life. Your child needs to know that you both are going to be there for him. He needs to be in a safe environment where he can adapt and grow into the trusting, caring individual that he is capable of being.

The starting place for all future changes in your child's world lies in the examples he or she chooses to copy. The more we learn, the more we understand that **your negative behavior will have a profound impact on your child's life.** It is your privilege and responsibility to help your child grow into a self-assured adult filled with understanding and a zest for life and it's many challenges.

We are all a part of something much bigger than ourselves. Acknowledging this fact is one key to changing our lives. First we come to terms with the presence of God, and then we place all the unmanageable aspects of our lives with Him. Be personally responsible in carrying out the directions you will receive. You have to be committed to follow through. It's the commitment and repetition that will give you the means to control what happens in the rest of your life.

After you explore and discover your mission, you will then have to decide whether or not you are willing to devote your life to it's completion. Respect the portion of God's spirit that was infused into your tiny body when you were resting in your mother's womb. At birth you were born in love, with all the essentials needed to accomplish your mission.

Realize that you will be held accountable for your lack of accomplishment while you inhabit your physical form on earth. Maximize your potential by rejecting chaos and accepting the serenity that "turning it over" brings. Get serious about your life. Whatever you do, make the commitment now and follow through!

If you establish a positive environment around your child you provide a certain range of protection for him. He will be less inclined to take up bad behaviors that could plague him for the duration of his life. If he is not internalizing negativity from a parent, his immune system will be stronger and he will be less likely to suffer from recurrent childhood episodes of illness such as chronic colds, viruses, and ear infections. Yes, believe it or not, your aura does have a profound effect in your child's life.

Involve your child early in the charitable endeavor of helping others. It is important not only to show your child love, but to also teach him or her the art of expressing love for his fellow man. Show by example the value of being a person who does not cast judgment but chooses instead to seek avenues for understanding and tries to help other people.

Teach him or her the futility of using aggression as a means to obtain approval or control over other people. Affirm that there is absolutely no room for violence in a happy home either between spouses or between parent and child. The old adage "violence begets violence" is still true today. Resist the temptation to express your feelings through anger and violence. This alone can destroy a child's sense of security and plant the pattern he will follow in his own future relationships. Through anger and violence you will insure that you will have a troubled teen who is inclined to lash out when faced with the many challenges and difficulties he will encounter.

Look through your child's eyes. Be in his corner as his most staunch supporter. Fulfill this important mission in life. Mold your child with care and serve as a guide. Your child is like a sponge ready to soak up your wisdom. We all made mistakes in our lives, but GOD in his infinite wisdom gives us another chance when he allows us to have and raise a precious child.

Take all the new found wisdom you have unearthed, and teach your child well. Teach your child a new better way to live. Insure that he will always feel good about himself by expressing the value you find in yourself. The ripple effect is always there. There is indeed some merit attached to the concept of cloning. Your child is waiting to grasp your every nuance. It will be difficult to put the brush to the canvas at times, but you must try. The child expects you to be the responsible person who is interested in his well being. Set clear rules and expectations and be consistent. Be understanding without going overboard. It is up to you, the adult, to separate the things your child wants to have or do from the things he needs. A child needs help establishing and adhering to a set of standards that will prove beneficial for a lifetime. With a set of healthy values in place, the child learns to resist the peer pressure to do the behaviors that are ultimately bad for his impressionable budding character. Balance peer pressure by keeping rules and regulations fair and reasonable. Deal with bad behavior as soon as you can without embarrassing your child in front of others. Be consistent in your response. Your children want guidance even when they are most resistant.

I can't stress enough the necessity that you encourage learning and education even from a young age. Make it a priority, not a maybe. Intelligence is an ally in the difficult teen age years when your child is making choices that can change the course his life will take.

Other ingredients are essential to curb negative behavior. These ingredients are family unity, and positive communication and feedback, coupled with life style changes that often require a leap in faith. You will be duly served to search your heart and embrace a better way to live yourself. **If you are going to talk the talk you have to walk the walk.** If you do not truly believe and try to live the life you want for your child, the child will see through your deception immediately. Don't send conflicting messages to your child. Both spiritual and educational influence in your home can only serve to direct your parenting in the right direction. Your child will be better equipped to handle potential problems such as drugs, alcohol, and premarital sex. During their teen years they are preparing a road map to help them handle their journey into the numerous relationships they will develop in the course of their lifetime. They need to foster relationships that will encourage and be supportive of a positive belief system with people who share like values.

Share your child's dreams. Help them recognize future possibilities. Help them fill their little wagons and teach them the difference between pushing and pulling the "wagon of their dreams". Motivation is much easier if a child is pulled toward a goal instead of pushing the child in a certain direction.

One final area that I want to mention involves a method that fulfills your child's need to establish a vital sense of history. This history is made up of all the important events that occur in the child's life. Photos of traditional family rituals give you a perfect example. Start a photo album that belongs to your child. One never gets too old to appreciate the preservation of these cherished memories. Little girls generally have some type hope chest that is used to store these childhood momentos. In a male child, a simple shoe box with a lid will do just fine.

Share the four questions and how important the answers are. Teach your child about the relationship between GOD and humanity by showing a strong faith yourself. Remember, everyone has a purpose for being here. Everyone also has the responsibility to find that purpose. Don't try to produce a purpose for your child, but share your knowledge of what a purpose means. Once your child has a purpose in his or her life, he/she can focus on the completion of that destiny. **If you set the example, you will never be sorry. You will know in your heart that you truly did the very best you could.** We daily set examples for not only your children, but all the people that we come into contact with. Pass your wisdom on to others. Every person is valuable and deserves to have the tools that will serve to guide them to a better life.

God bless you, and bless any help you can give in spreading the message contained in the four questions. You can be a shining example, and I have confidence that your light will shine very brightly with all the others who are determined to make this a better world.

Chapter Thirteen The importance of mission

The third important question life which deals with whether or not you will be happy, contented, and have peace of mind is question number three: *Why am I here?* This question attempts to get at the purpose of one's creation.

Even before God created you, He decided what role He wanted you to play during your life. He planned exactly how He wanted you to serve Him, and then He shaped you for those tasks. You are the way you are with all of your unique talents because you were made for a specific ministry.

"For I know the plans I have for you, says the Lord. They are plans for good and not for evil, to give you a future and a hope." Jeremiah 29:11 TLB.

The brain is not capable of holding two thoughts at the same time. If one concentrates on purpose or mission, then one does not concentrate on addiction. As the Bible says, one cannot serve two masters.

In order to be successful in treating any addiction, the individual must find out what his mission or purpose of creation is and then pursue it. Toward this end, I have been doing a 30 minute radio/ internet talk

show called : **Freedom from Addiction/*Share Your Mission/Truth Just Below the Surface*** for the last 25 years. You can catch it by going to freedomfromaddiction.libsyn.com. This is where you will find my podcast which is available 24/7 and is permanently archived.

Chapter Fourteen The Addictive Behaviors

The complicated structure of the physical world often leads us to think we are less than perfect. On one level this is true, but on another level, the spiritual level, we have come to understand that there is a part of us that is perfect and for which we need make no excuses. Often feelings of unworthiness and low self-esteem increase to a level that we start trying to fix the apparent problems we have manifested by treating them with negative (addictive) behaviors that are not good for us.

When a behavior becomes harmful to you, you know it's harmful, and you continue to use it, then you have entered into the trap of addiction. When you lose sight of your true worth and feel you are not good enough, you become easy prey for the negative, distorted, and temporary fixes that all addictions provide.

In the course of our limited human existence, we all have come to deal with addictions of various kinds. Now we either grow to a level of spiritual awareness where we question the validity of these behaviors or we totally lose sight of our inner beauty and the goodness with which we were born. One addictive behavior is not all that different from any other addictive behavior since they all originate from the same place and have the same cause. Since all addictive behaviors share a common cause, none are any better or worse than any others.

However, addictive behaviors have their own unique social identities in that society labels them and often penalizes the individual for the various side effects and complications which result from these behaviors.

There are as many addictive behaviors as Carter has little liver pills, but we are limited to discussing the ones that are most widely recognized and are the most prevalent while at the same time giving recognition to some newcomers.

Pornography. Pornography is defined as a representation of sexual behavior in books, pictures, statues, motion pictures, and other media that is intended to cause sexual excitement. The distinction between pornography (illicit and condemned material) and erotica (which is broadly tolerated) is largely subjective and reflects changing community standards.

Pornography may well be the number one male addiction in the country and many other parts of the world.

Here are some random facts about pornography: A new porn film is created in the United States every 39 minutes. Women like to watch lesbian porn more than straight sex. The 1988 People vs. Freeman court cases stated that adult film production, as long as it does not "hurt" others, was protected as free speech under the First Amendment. 20% of men and 13% of women admit to watching porn online at work. Pornography addiction is a behavioral addiction that causes serious negative consequences of physical, mental, social, and/or financial well-being.

It is estimated that the monetary size of the porn industry in the United States is 10-12 Billion dollars. Pornography revenue is larger than all professional basketball, baseball, and football franchises—combined. Porn revenue is more than the combined revenues of ABC, CBS, and NBC which is $6.2 billion. Twelve percent of all websites on the Internet are pornographic. Over 40 million Americans are regular visitors to porn sites. Around 70% of men aged 18-24 visit porn sites in a typical month. Child pornography generates around $3 billion annually. There are over 116,000 searches for "child pornography" every day. Every second the online porn industry makes over $3,000.

Every second, nearly 30,000,000 unique Internet users view porn. Nearly 2.5 billion emails per day are pornographic, which is 8% of all emails. Over 35% of all Internet downloads are pornographic. Nearly one in four Internet search queries are about porn (68 million a day). There are around 42 million porn websites. 25%-33% of those who watch Internet porn are women. Pornography makes up 30% of all the data transferred across the Internet.

A survey of Hilton, Marriot, Hyatt, Sheraton, and Holiday Inn hotels found that almost 70% of their room service profits came from porn movies.

The average age of first Internet porn exposure is 11 years old. Disseminating pornography to a minor is considered illegal in most U.S. states. The only remaining pornography taboo that is nearly universally unaccepted is child pornography.

Pornography is different from erotica. Erotica portrays sexuality in high-art which focuses on feelings and emotions. Pornography focuses on sex in a sensational manner and emphasizes the physical act to arouse a quick reaction. The distinction between porn and erotica is always shifting, because the very definition of pornography is subjective and contextual. An image may be considered erotic in one culture and condemned as pornographic in another.

Pornography is often divided into two categories: soft-core and hard-core. A work is hard-core if it includes graphic sexual activity, visible penetration, and unstimulated sex scenes. Soft-core porn typically contains nudity or partial nudity in sexually suggestive scenes, but does not include explicit sexual activity, penetration, or extreme fetishism.

Racism. What is the definition of racism? It is the belief that groups of humans possess different behavioral traits corresponding to physical appearance and can be divided based on the superiority of one race over another. It may also mean prejudice, discrimination, or antagonism directed against other people because they are of a different race or ethnicity. It is a belief that race is a fundamental determinant of human traits and capacities and that racial differences produce an inherent superiority of a particular race. Definitions anchor us in principles. This is not an insignificant point. We must do the basic work of defining the kind of people we want to be in language that is stable. Being anti-racist requires persistent self-awareness, constant self-criticism, and regular self-examination. Denial is the heartbeat of racism, beating across ideologies, races, and nations.

What is "covert" racism? It may masquerade as curiosity, concern, or kindness, so even do-gooders fall into this trap sometimes. Ask yourself these questions to find out if you may be guilty of covert racism. Did you ever act overly friendly to a person of another race to make sure you didn't seem biased? Do you have uncomfortable thoughts about a person's race, even if you don't verbalize them? Have you ever asked someone for advice about dating a person from their race? Have you ever made snap judgments about a person's preferences based solely on their race or ethnicity? Have you ever asked someone questions about their race as if they were a spokesperson for all other members? Have you noticed someone's race and acted differently in some way because of it? Sustained friendships with people of other races can break down covert racism.

Latino elites used racism in the past to justify the displacement and enslavement of the indigenous population, and these beliefs, along with the resentment created by the continued exploitation of indigenous land and labor, culminated in the Guatemalan Civil War (1960-1996). This is one example.

Another example is inherent and systemic in our country today. This racism is deep in our culture. Remember, there are 400 years to reckon with, and the longer an addiction is held the longer it takes to overcome. This kind of chronic trauma leads to increased substance use disorders.

What exactly is systemic racism, and how is it related to addiction? Individual racism is where the policies and practices of institutions result in excluding or promoting designated groups. This type of racism removes individual intent. Systemic racism manifests in either institutional racism or structural racism.

Individual racism is a spiritual disease. When a racist belief causes harm to you or to someone you love, (whether it is physical, emotional, or psychological), and you can't stop the behavior, you are addicted to it and you need treatment.

Gossiping. Two of the most dangerous words in the English language are "I heard." Gossip is a casual or unconstrained conversation or reports about other people, typically involving details that are not confirmed as being true. Gossip fits into the negative thinking category of addictive behaviors. Lying is gossip and gossip is lying. It is its first cousin. Millions of us thrive off of our own misconceptions and misassumptions. Gossip gives the lowest form of human a means of looking down on people by reducing them. But it's a fact that you can not build yourself up by putting someone else down. You can only build yourself up by lifting someone else.

Gossip has moved from entertainment to malevolence by spreading false knowledge. Gossip is cancer in every arena of our social order. When good is attempted, too often misinformation reverses those good efforts. Because of gossip and the associated connection to racism and mental illness it instigates harm. Truth is often buried deep.

Some people are born with an organic brain deficiency, but the vast majority of gossiping is learned, environmental, psychologically trauma based, or from undue influences in one's life.

Gossip plus prejudice often results in mental illness. Gossip can become delusional which then becomes bias. If you're harboring biases or prejudices, you are laying the foundation for your own mental illness.

It is not the lies that people tell about you that comprise the real problem. It is mostly the willingness of recipients to believe them. So many of us have become instigators of the gossip "virus" to the point where almost no one knows what the truth is about anymore. Truth is the enemy of gossip.

One of the elements that sustains gossip is that it amuses. When information, including humor, is not quite slander, but damaging just the same, it becomes slander by virtue of the damage it causes. A person's good reputation can be dismantled by gossip in moments.

Nazi information minister Goebbels once said that if you tell a lie to the people enough, they will believe it is the truth. It's the same way with gossip.

Gossip is in our DNA. It's the undiagnosed social virus of our time and of all time for that matter. For almost 75% of us, we gossip without even knowing it, spreading it like a virus. Some forms of gossip can, and do, kill lots of people like a dangerous virus.

It is in our nature to want to know things and be seen as an authority to some degree...a contributor to the true knowledge of humankind. Don't try to be the smartest or most vociferous person in the room, but always try to be the most truthful. A quiet whisper of truth will always be more important than the loudest lie.

Gossip sets the groundwork for many forms of racism and bias. The definition of racism or prejudice is to have a preconceived notion, or prejudgment of an individual, or a group. The definition of gossip is the delivery of distorted or untrue information. To be able to deliver distorted information or to produce any destructive action based upon the distortion, requires that the assailant have a bias against the truth, whether unwittingly or not.

Gossip-inspired racism has its roots in fear; we feel safer when people think the way we think, and when we know we're wrong, we need them to shield us.

It's not difficult to find people around the world who hate you just because you exist. Misunderstandings are the building blocks ultimately for war. For the most part, in terms of basic human wants and needs, humans are not that different from one another.

Most sane people want to live in peace, but religion, race, class, and culture get in the way, and of course, so do corrupt governments that deprive their people of their basic rights.

Concerning gossip, if you don't create the problem in the first place, bias doesn't result, and you retain a greater footing in the world of the "mentally together". You've heard the term "hold your tongue". When you feel the urge to spread a dubious story about anyone, don't!

One-third of our population has absolutely no idea as to what critical thinking is. For them, it is easy to be led down a garden path, albeit thorny and fraught with poison ivy. Critical thinking has to do with not accepting what people say without gathering evidence of truth.

We need to do what's right and tell the truth about ourselves and others even when they insist upon lying. Only 5% of the gossip you hear about someone is 100% true. Buddha said, "All that arises comes from our thoughts..." Now don't let misinformation and lies change your thoughts into words.

When you think about it, nearly every drama in which humans find themselves is loosely based on some form of misinformation. We are so taken in by our inability to differentiate between the entertainment of mere stories, and the damage of "thought bombs of gossiping", that we really aren't growing properly. To genuinely evolve we must learn how to at least filter out the gossip that visits us constantly.

The intent of gossip is to take pleasure in exacting meanness, vengeance, or self-satisfaction of being that person who knows more than others. Always try to tell your best truth and even if you don't succeed keep aiming for it.

If truth matters outside the home, it must matter within the home as well. Good parents everywhere are constantly reminding their children that it is not what they do when everyone's watching that matters as much as when no one's watching.

When we hear of any food contamination threat, the first thing we do is stop eating it. It's guilty before being proven innocent because we want to protect our families just in case the gossip is true. All you have to do is make people afraid and they tend to bend to your will. A good example is: a virus can kill you so wear a mask.

The first thing anyone should do with suspected gossip is to ask, is this true? Most people skip this step, because that would take all the fun away. The Internet is far more fiction than fact. The dopey encourage ideas that have no basis in truth which is then spread throughout the social media universe. It is human nature to listen to compelling information and wash it around in our psyche. If we build upon any unverified data we are starting down a sorry path.

Make a commitment to learning to verify data. Take a moment to understand what critical thinking is all about. Understanding is the first step. Understand critical thinking as opposed to its opposite... judging. When we make a judgment especially in the absence of facts, we are branding ourselves as biased. In this case, we insist that we're right in the absence of evidence. All a stupid idea requires are people stupid enough to believe it without question.

The key to the maliciousness of gossip is that it really only serves the needs of the original source. Everyone else is the messengers you're not supposed to shoot. As the gossip grows so grows the distortion.

What hurts so much especially for young teens (and others) who are sometimes driven to suicide, is that the misconception people hold about them is so different from who they know themselves to be. Gossip is most dangerous if you believe the distortions people say about you. Don't say mean things about other people, either behind their backs or, face-to-face.

There is no such thing as good or acceptable gossip because by its very nature to gossip is to lie and even little lies catch up with us eventually. "The acid you attempt to spill on others invariably splashes on your own self" (ancient Chinese adage). Martin Luther King once said, "In the end, we will remember not the words of our enemies but the silence of our friends." Henry Thomas Buckle said, "Great minds discuss ideas. Average minds discuss events. Small minds discuss people and often bully them.

A significant part of the preceding discussion was supplied with permission by my friend and colleague, Howard Bronson, who is a critically thinking philosopher of the first order, author, and counselor. His book is entitled "Speak Up: Our gossipy world and its connection to racism and mental illness."

Control [Co-dependency]. Co-dependency is an addictive behavior characterized by: A belief that my needs, my wants, my opinions, and my feelings are much less important than your needs, wants, opinions, and feelings. A Codependent becomes, over time willing to sacrifice personal values for love and approval of others.

Co-dependents have a diminished capacity to initiate, to participate in, or to maintain healthy, loving, intimate relationships with other people. They have a preoccupation with persons, places, and things which leads to personal neglect and/or painful consequences. Co-dependents are obsessed with controlling other people and their behavior. They feel they have great insight into what other people need and what is good for them, but they have very little insight into themselves. Co-dependents control or manipulate others because their lives are so out of control, and it seems that manipulation of others is the only way to get anything done.

A co-dependent often absorbs himself or herself in another's problems, perhaps in order not to have to deal with his or her own. These people care so deeply, (and often so destructively) about other people that they have forgotten how to care for themselves.

Co-dependents feel responsible for so much because those around them feel responsible for so little, and they are just taking up the slack.

Co-dependents haven't cornered the market on agony, but they have gone through their pain without the anesthetizing effects of alcohol or other drugs, and the pain that comes from loving someone who is in trouble can be profound.

Co-dependents look normal but don't feel normal, therefore it's easier to deny there's a problem even if the individual had a basic understanding of the illness, which is most commonly not the case. People who are affected by any addictive illness turn all those who deal with them, and want to rescue them from their situation into co-dependents.

Co-dependents, by their very nature, are benevolent. They are concerned and responsive to the needs of others. They have worried themselves sick about other people. They have tried to help in ways that didn't help. They have said yes when they meant no. They have tried to make others see things their way. They have bent over backwards to avoid hurting other people's feelings, and in so doing have hurt themselves. They have been afraid to trust their feelings. They have believed lies and then felt betrayed. They have wanted to get even and punish others. They have felt so angry they have wanted to kill. They have struggled for their rights while other people said they didn't have any.

The co-dependency addiction most commonly becomes habitual and self-perpetuating in the same manner as all other addictive behaviors. It is equally self-destructive, for while the co-dependent reacts to people who are destroying themselves, he or she develops behaviors which prevent peace, happiness, and contentment. It is just an illusion that one can control another's behavior. The actual truth is that the only person we have any ability to control or change is our-self, and you know how difficult that often is.

Co-dependency may be harder to understand than other addictions because it is a paradox. On the surface it appears that an addicted individual is depending on the co-dependent, yet in reality it is the co-dependent who is dependent on the addicted individual and is influenced and affected by his or her moods, behavior, or love.

Characteristically co-dependents have an over-developed sense of responsibility. It is easier for them to be concerned with others rather than themselves. This in turn enables them not to look too closely at their own faults.

Co-dependents "stuff" their feelings from traumatic childhoods. They have lost the ability to feel or express their feelings because it hurts too much. They are isolated from and afraid of people and authority figures. They have become addicted to approval and/or excitement (drama) and have lost their own identity in the process. They are frightened by angry people and *any* personal criticism. They judge themselves too harshly and have a low sense of self-esteem. They are dependent personalities who are terrified of abandonment. They will do anything to hold on to a relationship in order not to experience painful abandonment feelings which they received from living with people who were never emotionally there for them. They experience guilt feelings when they stand up for themselves instead of giving in to others. They confuse love and pity and tend to "love" people they can pity and rescue. They have either become chemically dependent, married a chemical dependent, or found another compulsive personality, such as a workaholic, to fulfill their compulsive needs.

A subset type of co-dependency addiction is sometimes called "Love Addiction." Those that know the pain of obsessive love, know the agony of wanting that which seems to elude one's grasp and not being able to give it up. There is passion. There is intensity, and the passion and intensity can drive one insane in the addictive need to win the love and companionship of another.

Peele explains that, "The ever present danger of the loved object's withdrawal creates an ever present craving for it." Those suffering from love addiction are paralyzed by the thought of the relationship ending and cannot cope with the possibility of its termination. Love addiction often results from the incorrect idea that someone else can make us whole, better, happier, more content, or in some manner improve our self-esteem and self-concept.

Substance Abuse. Substance abuse cost the United States more than

$740 billion a year on health care expenses, criminal justice, social welfare consequences, and lost work place productivity.

Many Americans stayed away from the emergency room when the nation went under lock-down for fear of contracting COVID-19 at the hospital. While this led to an overall decline in emergency department visits, a recent study shows weekly trips to the ER for drug overdoses were higher in 2020 than in 2019.

Researchers from the Centers for Disease Control and Prevention studied more than 180 million ER visits from Dec. 30, 2018, to Oct. 10, 2020, and found that weekly counts of all drug overdoses were up to 45% higher in 2020 than in 2019. Opioid overdoses, specifically, increased about 29% compared with before the pandemic.

Overall visits to the emergency room plummeted when COVID-19 lockdown measures were implemented in March 2020, decreasing about 43% compared with the same time frame in 2019. But drug overdoses experienced only a slight decrease from March 29 to April 11, about 4% compared with 2019, before increasing again.

Marijuana. Marijuana, also called pot, grass, or weed comes from the Cannabis Sativa plant which grows wild and is cultivated in many parts of the world. The plant contains over 400 chemicals and intoxicates primarily as a result of a psychoactive, mind altering substance called THC (delta-9 tetrahydrocannabinol). It is the THC content which is found in different parts of the plant at different concentrations that determines the potency of the marijuana. THC content is controlled by plant strain, climate, soil conditions, and harvesting.

Typically, marijuana is rolled into cigarettes (joints) made from dried particles of the plant excluding the main stem and roots. The tops generally have the highest THC concentration. Hashish (hash) is a green, dark brown or black resin extracted from the Cannabis sativa plant and is smoked to produce a high. Hash averages 2% THC.

Hash oil is a further modification with THC concentration running as high as 30%. Hash oil is a tar-like substance smoked in small amounts in cigarettes or in water pipes.

Physical effects include: increase in heart rate, reddening of the eyes, drying of the mucous membranes, a mild decrease in body temperature, and increased appetite("munchies").

Marijuana temporarily impairs short term memory, alters sense of time, and reduces the ability to perform tasks requiring coordination, swift reactions, and concentration. High doses have been known to induce hallucinations and produce image distortions.

Psychologically marijuana can cause paranoia and anxiety states. It does not directly cause mental problems but can unmask underlying defects.

Marijuana interferes with learning by impairing thought processes, decreasing reading comprehension, verbal, and arithmetic skills. It encourages a type of escapism which is harmful, especially in the adolescent, by separating him or her from the "growing pains" associated with learning to become a mature, responsible, and independent adult.

"Burn-out" is a syndrome associated with prolonged frequent use of the drug. It is characterized by a "laid back," apathetic, unambitious personality. The user is dull, slow moving, and inattentive. This syndrome may not be completely reversible even after prolonged abstinence from the drug.

Marijuana metabolites can be detected by common tests up to a week after the drug is smoked. Radioactive labeled THC tests can detect the metabolites for 4-5 weeks. THC is accumulated in fatty tissues such as the brain and these tissues give up the drug very slowly.

Marijuana has legitimate medical usages in treatment of glaucoma, for resistant nausea associated with cancer chemotherapy, for some seizures, and other conditions.

Marijuana has the same toxic effects on the lungs as does nicotine but in a ratio of up to 16:1.

Alcohol. It is estimated that over 15.7 million people in the U.S. Have alcohol use disorder. Annual health care cost are in excess of $225 billion and in terms of overall cost to our society. Alcohol abuse and dependency and the many problems that come with it affect every neighborhood, work place, school, and family. Experience shows that at least four other people are affected by the behavior of each alcoholic. A large survey found excessive drinking as the fourth most worrisome personal problem in this country.

The Institute of Medicine has reported that, among adults, 20% of the people have major problems because of their drinking and 70-80% of all Americans are alcohol consumers. Alcohol lowers the life expectancy by 12 years on the average, and is the number one killer of young people between the ages of 15 and 24 in alcohol related traffic accidents. It is responsible for 1/3 of all suicides, 1/2 of murders and traffic deaths, and 1/4 of all other accidents.

Alcohol, the major ingredient in wine, beer, and distilled liquor, is a natural substance formed by the reaction of fermenting sugar with yeast spores. The kind of alcohol found in alcoholic beverages is ethyl alcohol, a colorless, flammable liquid with an intoxicating effect. It produces a feeling of well-being, sedation, intoxication or unconsciousness, depending on the amount consumed.

A half ounce of pure alcohol is found in a 12 ounce beer, 5 ounces of wine, or a 1 ounce-86 proof cocktail. The body can metabolize 1/4 of an ounce of pure alcohol per hour in an average sized (250 pound) individual.

The effects of alcohol are dose related. They include impaired vision, distorted depth perception, slurred speech, poor coordination, reduced problem solving ability, mood swings, memory impairment, and poor judgment. Alcohol is a depressant, and as drinking continues, can cause death by depressing the cardiac and respiratory centers of the brain.

Hallucinogens. Hallucinogens, or psychedelics, are drugs that alter a person's perceptions, sensations, thinking, self-awareness, and emotions. They include such drugs as LSD, mescaline, psilocybin, DMT, and PCP. The effects are unpredictable and depend on the amount taken, the type of drug, the personality of the user, and the mood, expectations, and surroundings in which the drug is used. Usually the user feels the effect of a hallucinogen within 30-90 minutes after taking it.

Physical effects include dilated pupils, hyperthermia, increased heart rate and blood pressure, sweating, loss of appetite, dry mouth, sleeplessness, and tremors.

Sensations and feelings change too. The user may feel several different emotions at once or swing rapidly from one emotion to another. The person's sense of time and self changes. Sensations may "cross-over" giving the user the feeling of "hearing" colors and "seeing" sounds. These hallucinations can he very frightening and include a state of panic.

These drugs can unmask an underlying mental or emotional problem which was previously unknown. Flashbacks, in which a person experiences a drug's effect without taking the drug again can occur.

Heavy or chronic use can cause signs of organic brain damage with impaired memory and attention span, mental confusion, and difficulty with abstract thinking.

LSD is manufactured from lysergic acid, which is found in ergot, a fungus that grows on rye and other grains. LSD, discovered in 1938, is one of the most powerful mood changing chemicals. It is odorless, colorless, and tasteless.

LSD is sold on the streets in tablets, capsules, or occasionally in liquid form. It is usually taken by mouth, but occasionally it is injected. Often it is added to absorbent paper, such as blotter paper and divided into small decorated squares, with each square representing a dose.

Mescaline comes from the peyote cactus and although it is not as strong as LSD, its effects are similar. Mescaline is usually smoked or swallowed in the form of capsules or tablets.

Psilocybin comes from certain mushrooms. It is sold in tablet or capsule form for oral ingestion. The mushrooms themselves, fresh and dried, can be eaten.

DMT is another psychedelic drug that acts like LSD. Its effect begins almost immediately but only lasts 30-60 minutes.

PCP (phencyclidine) is also known as "angel dust". It has hallucinogenic properties but also can relieve pain and act as a stimulant. It was first introduced as an anesthetic in the 1950's. However it was withdrawn from the market because of its side-effects. PCP is easily manufactured. However, users can never be sure of what they are buying since it is made in illegal labs. PCP is available in a number of forms. It can be a pure, white crystalline powder, a tablet, or a capsule. It can be swallowed, smoked, sniffed, or injected. PCP is sometimes sprinkled on marijuana or parsley and smoked. Physical effects include increased heart rate and blood pressure, flushing, sweating, dizziness, and numbness. In large doses effects include drowsiness, convulsions, and coma. Death sometimes results from repeated convulsions, heart and lung failure, or stroke.

PCP can produce violent or bizarre behavior in people who are not normally that way. PCP effects memory, perception, concentration, and judgment. Users may show signs of paranoia, fearfulness, and anxiety. Some users become aggressive, others withdraw. Temporary mental disturbance of thought processes (PCP psychosis) may last days to weeks.

Opiates (Narcotics). Opiates are a group of drugs which are used medically for pain relief. They also have a high abuse potential. Some opiates come from the resin of the Asian poppy. This group of drugs includes opium, heroin, morphine, and codeine. Other opiates such as Demerol (meperidine) are synthetic and are manufactured.

Opiates tend to relax the user. When injected the user feels an immediate "rush". Other initial and unpleasant effects often include restlessness, nausea, and vomiting. The user may go "on the nod", going back and forth between feeling alert and being drowsy. With very large doses (OD), the user can not be awakened, pupils constrict, and skin becomes cold, moist, and bluish in color, breathing slows down, and death may occur. Tolerance develops in this class of drugs requiring higher and higher doses to produce the same effect. Problems associated with IV use include AIDS, hepatitis, and infections.

Physical withdrawal is often severe and usually starts 4-6 hours after the last dose. Symptoms include uneasiness, diarrhea, abdominal cramps, chills, sweating, nausea, and runny nose and eyes. The intensity of the symptoms depends on the dosage, frequency, and duration of use. Symptoms peak in 1-3 days and resolve in 7-10 days. However drug craving commonly lasts for months.

Opium is usually seen as dark brown chunks or as a powder and is usually smoked or taken by mouth.

The most commonly abused drug in this category is heroin. Heroin, a white to brownish powder is usually injected, smoked, or snorted. Since 2001 heroin use has increased well over 500%. Heroin dependence has more than tripled. Heroin has increased greatest among white males and those with lower income and education.

Dilaudid and Demerol are used IV or taken in pill form by mouth. Codeine and hydrocodone preparations are taken orally. Morphine is used both IV and orally. Methadone, a synthetic opiate, does not produce the same heroin high and blocks craving for that drug. However, it is addicting in its own right.

Inhalants. Inhalants are drugs that produce psychoactive vapors. They include solvents, aerosols, some anesthetics, and other chemicals. Examples are model airplane glue, gasoline, toluene, spray paints, cookware coating agents, hair sprays, nitrous oxide, medical skin coolants, and nitrites.

Inhalant effects include nausea, coughing, nosebleeds, malaise, bad breath, loss of coordination, loss of appetite, ringing of the ears, and alteration of judgment. There is often a decrease in heart and respiratory rates. At increased doses one may lose touch with one's surroundings, lose self-control, develop violent behavior, or become unconscious. When unconsciousness is associated with vomiting, often asphyxiation and death follows. Chronic problems associated with long term use include damage to liver, kidneys, blood, and bone marrow.

Amyl nitrite is a clear, yellowish liquid sold in cloth-covered, sealed bulbs. When the bulb is broken it makes a snapping sound, thus they are referred to as "snappers"or "poppers". Amyl nitrite has been used in the past for cardiac patients. When it became only available by prescription in 1979, many abusers switched to butyl nitrite.

Butyl nitrite is packaged in small bottles and sold under a variety of names such as "locker room" and "rush". It produces a high that lasts from a few seconds to several minutes. The immediate results include decreased blood pressure, followed by an increased heart rate, flushed face and neck, dizziness and headache.

Depressants. "Downer" is the street name for this class of drugs which include tranquilizers, sleeping pills, and barbiturates. Alcohol is also a "downer." Barbiturates include seconal, tuinal, amytal, reds, rainbows, Mexican reds, "amies", barbs, and blues.

Depressants function to slow down or depress the activity of the brain, heart, lungs, nerves, and muscles. They result in a calm, relaxed, sleepy feeling. Drugs in this class are dangerous in high dosages, especially when combined with alcohol because of potentiation (increased effect over two drug's individual effects) and have resulted in many deaths. They have a significant dependency potential and have been associated with withdrawal seizures.

Hypnotics. Examples are Restoril, Dalmane, Halcion, and others. Methaqualones are no longer legally manufactured but include Quaaludes, Mequin, Spoors, Ludes, and 714s.

Tranquilizers. Examples include Xanax, Valium, Librium, Tranzene, and Ativan.

Methamphetamine. Methamphetamine is sold under the pharmaceutical brand name, Desoxyn. Methamphetamine (crystal-meth) produces an intense wave of physical psychological exhilaration upon injection. This wave of pleasure is, of course, known as a "rush". The drug's euphoric effects are similar to but longer lasting than cocaine. The rush associated with crystal-meth is an extremely potent reinforcer and directly associated with its addictive potential. Dangers associated with crystal-meth are similar to those of amphetamines in general and for those "running" the drug, complications include: infection, AIDS, hepatitis, and OD's. Crystal-meth effectively erases the feeling of hunger and fatigue. "Speed" users are able to overload their systems for long periods of time, creating the same sort of stress demands that follow a marathon run. But unlike the runner who rests after the stress, the crystal-meth user often forges on, for days and weeks at a time, without rest and usually without food, placing impossible demands on the body.

Ice, crystal, glass, quartz, and ALA are street names for the smokeable form of crystal-meth. It is a large, usually clear crystal of high purity (generally greater than 90%) which is generally smoked in a glass pipe. The drug is almost exclusively used by this route. The smoke is odorless and the residue from the drug stays in the pipe and can be smoked a second time.

Methamphetamine abuse in this form is associated with psychosis, violent behavior, and seizures. Cardiovascular effects include arrhythmia, strokes, chest pains,"heart attacks," elevated blood pressure, palpitations, and elevated heart rates. When elevated body temperature (hyperthermia) results from drug use, breakdown of muscle (rhabdomyolisis) and kidney damage may follow. Mortality rates are as high or higher than those produced by smoking "crack." The high produced by "ice" is comparable to that produced by "crack," but the effects may last up to ten times as long. Withdrawal from methamphetamine use is not associated with physical signs, but drug craving, depression, sleepiness, and hunger are often seen.

Methamphetamine's My Name-Destruction My Game.

My name is methamphetamine....call me Meth for short.

I entered this country sans a passport.

And every since then I've made lots of scum rich.

Some have been murdered and found in a ditch.

I'm more valued than diamonds, more treasured than gold.

Use me just once and you too will be sold.

I'll make a schoolboy forget his books.

I'll make a beauty queen forget her looks.

I'll make a schoolteacher forget how to teach.

I'll make a preacher not want to preach.

I'll take all your money and you'll be evicted.

I'll murder your babies or they'll be born addicted.

I'll make you lie, rob, steal, and kill.

When you're under my power you will have no will.

Remember, "my friend", my name is "Meth".

If you try me one time, it may mean your death.

I've destroyed politicians and many a hero.

I've decreased bank accounts from millions to zero.

I make shooting and stabbing a common affair.

Once I take charge of your life you won't have a prayer.

Now that you know me, what will you do?

You'll have to decide it's all up to you.

Today you decide will you sit in my saddle?

The decision is one that no one can straddle.

Listen to me and please listen well.

When you ride with Meth you're riding to Hell!

Ectasty. is also known on the street as "X-TC" and "Adam". All three are names for the psychoactive drug, MDMA. MDMA has hallucinogenic and amphetamine like properties. Ecstacy users claim MDMA can cause people to trust one another and break down barriers between therapists and clients. MDMA's use has escalated with college students and young adults who frequent all night dance parties called "raves." Problems encountered with MDMA are: confusion, depression, drug craving, anxiety, paranoia (MDMA selectively damages serotonin neurons), muscle tension, involuntary teeth clenching, nausea, blurred vision, and increased heart rate and blood pressure.

Crank. is the time honored street name for speed like pharmaceutical amphetamines, white crosses, and various bootlegged amphetamines. Since most often this form of amphetamine is ingested orally, the dangers are not as acute as crystal or ice. Still crank stresses the body both physically and psychologically.

Delusional states and toxic psychotic states like paranoid schizophrenia can result from heavy, even short-term, use.

Amphetamines increase the heart rate and blood pressure, dilate the pupils, and decrease appetite. They can cause dry mouth, sweating, headache, blurred vision, dizziness, sleeplessness, and anxiety. There is an association with this drug use and stroke, hyperthermia, and heart failure. Dependency and tolerance (the need to take increasingly higher doses) routinely accompany continued use. Abrupt withdrawal may precipitate seizures.

Cocaine. Cocaine is a white powder that comes from the leaves of the coca plant. Users call it by a variety of names including coke, C, snow, blow, toot, nose candy, and lady. The street drug is a combination of cocaine and "cut" (an adulterate that increases the volume and therefore the seller's profit). Crack is cocaine processed into a "free-base" form so it can be smoked. Formally ether was used to accomplish this conversion, but because of the danger using a highly flammable solvent, now more commonly heat and baking soda are employed.

The product: crack, contains some impurities and excess baking soda. When heated the mixture, which looks like small lumps of soap but has the consistency of porcelain, makes a crackling sound. It is often referred to "rock" or "ready-rock."

Cocaine users most commonly "snort" the drug. Later cocaine is sometimes injected in a water based solution or smoked in a water pipe in the form of crack. Both of these methods are more rapidly addictive than "snorting." Physical effects of cocaine and crack include dilated pupils, and vasospasm (narrowing of the blood vessels), increased blood pressure and heart rate, breathing rate, and body temperature.

Users lose their appetites and are unable to sleep. Individuals who "snort" the drug have a runny nose. Initially cocaine elevates the mood and gives the user a sense of well-being and exhilaration. When injected or smoked, crack produces one of the most ecstatic "highs" imaginable within seconds. Cocaine effects wear off rapidly and the user slips into a "let down" depression with feelings of dullness, tenseness, edginess, and an intense drug craving (of a psychological nature). By virtue of the cardiovascular effects that the drug has on the body, heart attacks, strokes, and sudden death are not unlikely complications of its use. They are not necessarily dose related and can result from occasional or low-dose use. Convulsions are another relatively commonly seen side-effect. Those using cocaine intravenously suffer from the same risk of AIDS, hepatitis, and infections associated with other IV drug users. Scarring from injections leave noticeable "tracks". Psychological effects of cocaine and crack use include violent, erratic, and paranoid behavior. These "cocaine psychoses" appear more rapidly in those who smoke or inject the drug.

Hallucinations are also common. Intense drug seeking behavior results from overwhelming feelings coming from the brain's "pleasure center". This behavior is referred to as "Jonesing". Other psychological personality changes occur with chronic, daily use or "binges". Thinking is impaired, and users become confused, anxious, and depressed. Tempers are often short, panic attacks common, and suspiciousness frequently characterizes relationships with friends, loved ones, and co-workers. Continued use can cause a partial or total break with reality. Combining cocaine and heroin (speed ball) or PCP (space base) increases risk of death through physical and psychological complications dramatically.

Sexual performance is adversely effected by use of this class of drug. Males most commonly find impotence and delayed ejaculation as side effects. Most women have difficulty reaching orgasm. Still, cocaine has a reputation of being the easiest way of attracting desirable women for sexual purposes. It is ironic that drug's use often becomes more desirable in the user's mind than the sexual partner.

Anabolic Steroids. Anabolic steroids are synthetic derivatives of the male hormone testosterone. They promote muscle growth, increase strength, and potentiate the development of male sex characteristics. Steroids of this type have been used in medicine to promote weight gain in patients who have undergone major surgery, in certain bone diseases, and anemias. Anabolic steroids are rarely used in medicine these days but commonly used on the street by weight lifters, bodybuilders, power track athletes, and even some sprint athletes to increase muscle mass, strength, and explosive power. Athletes use the drug to increase their self-image and to win...often at a great cost. A real tragedy has begun to take hold in the non-athlete who uses anabolic steroids to increase his size, strength, and aggressive behavior patterns in order to compete in our society where good looks and aggressiveness often seem more important than intelligence or morality.

Most anabolic steroid abusers obtain anabolic steroids from the "black market" as these drugs have become D.E.A. scheduled and doctors are more and more refusing to dispense them. Yet up to 20% of users report physicians, pharmacists, or veterinarians as their primary provider. Anabolic steroids may be taken orally or by injection. Steroid abusers typically run through self treatment schedules called either "pyramiding" or "stacking". A pyramid begins with low doses of one steroid. Dosages are increased and other steroids stacked on top of the primary drug to typically produce over 100 times the medically indicated dosage. Typically the anabolic steroid user, in a 12 week cycle, will pyramid and stack drugs through the 5th to 7th week and then reverse the process. After the 12 week cycle, the abuser will often observe a drug free period to "clean out" his system. After this time of getting clean a new cycle begins.

Physical side effects of anabolic steroids use include early closure of the growth plates creating short stature, the development of impotency, male infertility, and permanent development of male sexual characteristics in the female user.

Psychological side effects include aggressive behavior, increased energy, and increased libido. Adolescents may be even more sensitive to the effect. Evidence of rage attacks and paranoia have been linked to the overuse of anabolic steroids.

Liver disorders, including malignant tumors, cysts, and jaundice have been reported in steroid users. Cardiovascular complications include high blood pressure and profound decrease in the protective cholesterol (HDL). This may explain reports of increased heart disease in National Football League alumni.

Other side effects include acne, increased skin and hair oiliness, male pattern baldness, and hirsutism (increased hair growth). There may also be an increased tendency toward blood clotting which could increase the chance of stroke. It has been estimated that 10% of all high school seniors have used anabolic steroids for psycho-social reasons. This is particularly disturbing as anabolic steroids result secondarily in increased self-esteem so well and at the same time are so potentially damaging to the chronic adolescent user.

Gambling. The gambling addiction draws from two other addictions: greed and excitement. On one hand it evolves from incorrect thinking that there is an easy way of short-circuiting the normal progression of things and that one can "get something for nothing." On the other hand there is that sense of adventure and excitement in the uncertainty of winning or losing over the turn of a card or the roll of the dice. Many gambling addicts feel a "rush" just as they realize they have won the bet. This is often not related to the monetary gain. The feeling is comparable to the high induced by certain drugs and to the sensation experienced just as a kleptomaniac starts to steal something.

Excessive Computer/TV/SmartPhone Use. The average American spends 49 days each year on their screens. The average American picks up their phone 80 times a day. "I am pretending to talk to you but I am sneaking a down look at my screen."

"Surfing the net" is a new addiction beginning in the nineties which continues and increases as time goes on. While it has some similarities to the addictive behavior of excitement manifested in the television compulsion of watching soap operas, internet surfing is distinct in it's own right. In Kimberly Young's study of 400 individuals with exaggerated computer use, she found that their compulsion caused them to sneak online in the middle of the night and to stay home from work to "surf."

A news story told about a 24 year old woman living in Cincinnati, whose marriage broke up because of her addiction to her computer and specifically to the vast amount of time she spent on the internet. [She spent up to 12 hours a day online.] As though this side effect of the disease process wasn't bad enough, she was later arrested for child neglect and had her three children, ages 2, 3, and 5 removed from the home by child protective services. The mother would lock the children in their room so she would not be bothered. Their playroom had broken glass, debris, and children's hand prints in human feces on the walls. The house was in shambles, but the area around the computer was clean . . . really immaculate.

As a result of the compulsive behavior of excessive computer use, normalacies for time and space disappear. Much the same can be said for the individuals who are obsessively dependent on their televisions and smart phones.

Kleptomania. Kleptomania is an addictive impulse to steal without economic motive. This lack of economic motive is the chief characteristic that separates this subclass of addict from that of a common thief who also steals on a recurring basis but for different reasons. Addicts of this type are more often women than men because they have an intimate relationship to shopping that men don't usually possess. A shoplifter once remarked, "There's nothing quite like it. You haven't experienced the ultimate high until you've shoplifted on Rodeo Drive. For me it's better than sex." Most kleptomaniacs have a weird, euphoric feeling that comes over them just as they realize they are going to steal, and the "afterglow" can last up to days. The reward comes not from what was stolen, but rather in doing the act and getting away with it. It has been estimated that economic losses, just from stolen merchandise alone, in this country exceeds 6 billion dollars a year.

Smoking. Nicotine is the addictive psychoactive substance found in cigarettes. Nicotine dependence is the most common form of chemical dependency in the United States. Cigarette smoking is the number one cause of preventable death in our country and kills more Americans than alcohol, heroin, crack cocaine, AIDS, car accidents, and murder combined. It is a major health risk with proven associations to lung cancer, chronic obstructive lung disease (emphysema and chronic bronchitis), and heart disease.

If you smoke more than one pack of cigarettes a day, you're three times as likely to die of a heart attack than if you didn't smoke or if you quit smoking. If you smoke 5 cigarettes a day you are five times as likely to die of lung cancer. If you smoke 30 cigarettes daily, you are thirty times as likely to die from this disease.

The effects of chronic lung disease are proportional to the length and frequency of cigarette smoking and the damage is permanent and not significantly reversible by the cessation of smoking. Annual health care costs from the use of tobacco is in excess of $130 billion.

E-cigarettes have cartridges filled with liquid nicotine, flavors, and other chemicals. The assessment of all of the health hazards has not been fully evaluated in adults. Smoking E-cigarettes is known as vaping. Drug users are increasingly using E-cigarettes to vape illicit drugs such as marijuana, heroin, methamphetamine, and others. Liquid nicotine used in E-cigarettes can be fatal to a child in doses of 1/2 teaspoon and up. The liquid sold to vape stores is between two and 6 teaspoons in a bottle. It comes in a variety of nicotine strengths. A teaspoon of concentrated liquid nicotine can be fatal to a 26 pound toddler.

Sociopathic Behavior. This sub-class of addiction doesn't fit the medical model as well as the others, but in as much as the cause of this behavior is the same as the others, if any treatment is going to work this would be it. To date there is no other routinely successful treatment. Individuals exhibiting this type of behavior have been around for centuries. They were thought to suffer from "moral insanity" in the 1880's. Around the turn of the century they were termed "psychopaths". By the 1960's, when psychiatrists tied social conditions to their behavior, they became known as "sociopaths." Most recently these people have been diagnosed as having an "antisocial personality disorder or narcissistic personality disorder."

What ever you call these individuals, they are people with no loyalty who obey only their own desires. They are unpredictable and lack any real connection or attachment to others. They use, abuse, and manipulate others for the sheer pleasure of it. One of the most frightening aspects of this type of personality is that these people operate under a guise or mask of sanity.

Characteristically these people are: intelligent, charming, devoid of feelings of guilt, shame, or remorse and are unable to learn from their experiences. They lack in the ability to feel fear for themselves, are impulsive and unpredictable. They are often unreliable and insincere. They lie while conveying the impression of deepest sincerity and truthfulness. They are narcissistic and incapable of feeling real love for others.

Compulsive liars may or may not be sociopaths. Although compulsive lying is a characteristic of this sub-group, there are many more things that go into diagnosing this condition as has been previously noted. When a sociopath is caught in a lie, he or she tries to cover up with another lie or fakes repentance until forgiveness is obtained.

The major reason for lack of treatment success comes from the very characteristics of this diseased personality which contribute to complete, persistent denial. Most true sociopaths never break through the denial to recognize their need for treatment.

Overeating and Undereating. Statistics show that in 2018, 31% of adult Americans were obese meaning that a body mass index was higher than 30. 35% of young adults, 43% of middle-aged adults, and 41% of older adult are obese. One reason for this is easier access to unhealthy food. Also high calorie fattier foods can be purchased cheaper. Prices for healthy foods have increased at a faster rate than non-healthy foods. On average obese adults spend 42% more on healthcare than healthy adults.

One form of under-eating is known as Anorexia Nervosa, a condition affecting females with a frequency 10 times that of males. Generally beginning in adolescence, there is often spontaneous remission by the late twenties unless death intervenes in the mean-time. The mortality rate has been estimated as high as 10%. An addictive desire to lose weight is the basis for this condition which is often associated with other compulsive abuses in the areas of exercise, diuretics (fluid pills), and laxatives. Many anorexics paradoxically binge in spite of their desire to be thin.

Bulemia is another eating condition which is also more prevalent in females and begins during adolescence. Bulemics have binge and purge cycles and often self-induce vomiting after eating. As opposed to anorexics who are typically underweight, bulemics tend to be normal or slightly overweight.

Compulsive over-eating is a symptom of addiction common to a large percentage of the population. Over-eating is now in the top three most common addictive behaviors in the country. The severity of the addictive craving varies from individual to individual, but there is little appreciation for taste, texture, or the amount of food ingested. Binge eaters are predominately women with an average age of 42 who most likely developed food problems before the age of 10. Most binges last from 15 minutes to one hour, occur 2 times a day, and contain 1600 calories each time, according to a national survey.

Sexual and Non-Sexual Abuse. Abuse is a major problem in this country. Most abusers whether it be child abusers, spouse abusers, or abusers of the aged, are not sadistic humans getting delight out of the pain they inflict. They, like all the other sub-groups of addicts, are people who are compulsively out of control. Whether the abuse is sexual or non-sexual, of children or the elderly, psychological or physical, it is all the same. The same environmental factors have worked on abusers as on all the rest of us, except there is a higher incidence of abusers having been abused themselves. With that "tape" in their memory, they are more likely to react under stress with psychological, emotional, or physical violence. Abuse patterns develop from low self-esteem and inadequate consciousness, just like all the other addictive behaviors and are rooted in frustration, guilt, shame, and self-doubt. Most abusers, having also been abused, never developed adequate coping skills.

Workaholism. The addictive need to overwork, especially at one's occupation, has not been appreciated to be a very "bad" addiction by most people. We accept the positive idea that "work is good" on which our Puritan work ethic was founded. However, if we stop to critically evaluate the situation, we can see that bad side-effects and complications follow overwork just as they do in all the other addictions. This addiction is characterized by working long hours, working on weekends, skipping vacations, and is generally task orientated rather than performance or goal orientated. Workaholics are more commonly men than women because job success is central to a man's identity and men have been taught that success at work should be their primary goal in life. Women have been traditionally taught more often than not that the family should be their success goal and therefore they are not represented as frequently in this sub-class of addictions.

There is little difference between the salesman who is gone 150 nights a year, but only needs to work 100 nights to adequately provide for himself and his family, and the housewife who attends every community help project because she can't say no.

There is of course a difference between a permanent work addiction and similar behavior motivated by a short term goal of reaching a certain level of accomplishment. In both cases, the behavior may look exactly the same, but if the desired result is a defined level of success, when this is reached the excessive work behavior ends.

Workaholics hurt themselves. The stress, tension, and fatigue caused by their addiction wears out their bodies prematurely causing heart attacks, strokes, and any number of other illnesses. Workaholics also hurt their families and loved ones by destroying and damaging relationships due to their absence and by lack of motivation and energy when they are present.

Excitement. The excitement addiction is the compulsive need to engage in behavior which often adds an element of danger or risk to one's life. While this is most obvious with respect to some types of behavior like race car driving, mountain climbing, and parachuting, it also is present in behavior like playing video games, watching soap operas, and sports competition. Obviously the bad side effects and complications of this subgroup vary considerably depending on the type of behavior.

Power and Greed. Greed and the pursuit of power, fame, prestige, social standing, and hedonism are all parts of this sub-class of addictions. Greed can be defined as self interest out of control. There is a sacrifice of personal integrity and strict compliance with the law for the sake of immediate profit and/or accumulating money or material possessions. Hedonism can develop into an addiction of pleasure seeking, a constant search to be involved only with things that feel good. The pursuit of power can be a totally encompassing addiction, which has led to some of the largest tragedies the world has known. All war has its basis, at least partially, in power addictions. Similar to power needs are needs of fame, prestige, and social standing.

Power is exercising

One's own free will.

And power is dangerous

'cause power can kill.

We most want it when

We think that we lack

And feigning esteem

Freedom From Addiction 4

Won't take up the slack.

Power lust is contagious.

It spreads like wildfire.

It flames the emotions

Causing men to aspire

To control of the masses,

To control of free will.

It moves and excites them

And provides such a thrill

That it quickly addicts them,

And then they can't stop

This wrong way of thinking,

Even if they could swap

It for something better.

If they could let go

And not need control

Their spirits could grow.

But the past teaches sadly

That power's great sin

Is the damage it does

To our fellow men.

Yes the past teaches sadly

That power's a curse

If it were different

We'd not need this verse.

Teenage Rebellion. I often refer to this as "drugs, sex, and rock-and-roll." Any parent of teenagers is well aware of the behavioral characteristics we are discussing in this sub-segment. While teenage rebellion may not follow the addictive model as well as some of the other addictive behaviors, it's cause is the same as all the other addictions and the condition responds to therapy in the same way.

Sexual Compulsions. The most common sexual compulsions are rape, satyrism, and nymphomania. Rape is also a crime of power and aggression as well as a sexual addiction. Satyrism and nymphomania are older terms that refer to compulsive sexual relations by men and women, respectively. Homosexuality often takes on a compulsive nature with respect to the sexual act. It has been estimated that between 2-10 % of Americans are sex addicts.

Paraphilias are unconventional objects or situations that cause sexual arousal in some people and can be addictive in nature.

Fetishism—The reliance on a non-human object as the preferred method of achieving sexual excitement.

Voyeurism—The desire to watch others nude or having sexual relations.

Exhibitionism—The desire to expose one's genitals in public to achieve sexual arousal.

Transvestism—Dressing in the clothes of the opposite sex to achieve sexual gratification.

Masochism—Obtaining sexual gratification through being abused or dominated by another.

Sadism—Obtaining sexual satisfaction by abusing or dominating another.

Zoophilia (Beastiality)- Obtaining sexual gratification using animals as the preferred or exclusive sex object.

Pedophilia—Obtaining sexual gratification with children as the preferred or exclusive sex object.

Necrophilia—Obtaining sexual gratification with the dead as the preferred or exclusive sex object.

LGBTQIA+ . If you're just learning about sexuality, gender, and all these other things, they can be a little hard to remember. This acronym not only serves as a symbol of the movement for individual rights, but even as a memory tool for those who need help.

L- Lesbian is a term used to refer to homosexual females.

G- Gay is a term used to refer to homosexuality, a homosexual person, or a homosexual male.

B- Bisexual is when a person is attracted to two sexes/genders.

T-Trans is an umbrella term for transgender and transsexual people.

Q-Queer is an umbrella term for all of those who are not heterosexual and/or cisgender. Cisgender (sometimes cissexual, or shortened to *cis*) describes a person whose gender identity matches their sex assigned at birth. Questioning is when a person isn't 100% sure of their sexual orientation and/or gender, and are trying to find their true identity.

I-Intersex is when a person has an indeterminate mix of primary and secondary sex characteristics.

A-Asexuality is when a person experiences no or little sexual attraction to people.

The "+" symbol simply stands for all of the other sexualities, sexes, and genders that aren't included in these few letters. What percentage of people are LGBTQ+? I'm seeing estimates between 3% and 5% generally.

Overspending. Overspending is an addictive symptom which is more common in women than men, primarily because women are more intimately connected to shopping as a release for their frustrations of day to day living. They also get more pleasure out of shopping than the average male. This addiction is manifested in buying things that are not needed, buying more than is needed, and buying more frequently than needed. The "high" other addicts get in drugs is often approximated by buying that brand new sports car or the overpriced diamond necklace.

Overspending addicts suffer from bad side effects of overextended credit and ISF checks on a much higher frequency than others. This addiction often causes a myriad of financial and interpersonal relationship problems.

Negative Thinking. For many people negative thinking has become become an addiction. The effects of negative thinking can set off the "fight or flight" response which causes an adrenaline outpouring into the bloodstream. For some, like the excitement addiction, this becomes an addictive high. The mind can become involved by always being "right" about predicting failure, and predicting failure is the best way to guarantee failure will occur.

Emotions are involved with negative thinking and the stimulation it produces gives the "pay-off".....satisfying some of the symptoms in the addiction cycle, e.g. emptiness and boredom.

There are 12 common types of negative thinking: judging other people, refusing to trust, pessimism, fearing, chronic hopelessness, depreciating oneself or others, unwarranted defensiveness, complaining, whining, suffering, and gossiping.

You've often heard "pain-and-suffering" as if they were joined at the hip. But many spiritual writers have said that one has nothing to do with the other and we should separate them. In this book I am separating them. Both can be symptoms of the disease. Pain, of various types, is inevitable in life but suffering is an option. At the core of every underlying addictive behavior is suffering. When you wake up each morning you have the choice of obsessing about what's wrong with your life and suffering. However if you realized how blessed you are, you have a much higher chance of not suffering that day. Suffering can be an unconscious habit or when we are aware of it it can be an addiction to avoid.

I can relate to how suffering can be a curse or a joy. (Read chapter 15). In those days I was suffering, but I was also joyous in that I knew that this suffering came on as a result of a fulfilling a higher purpose. That purpose was to complete my writing a book on addiction. Even though I could count only 15 things that I possessed, I was happier than in the days when I was earning $50,000 per month. Unbelievable!

If you spend time around a negative thinker, you are in the presence of an energy and creativity vampire. My best advice is to leave the situation.

Collectoholism. When I wrote the original book, I had not had any collectaholic clients. However, subsequently it came to my attention that some people had an addictive urge to collect and hold on to things, collections, and material objects. Some did this with a passion and could not stop availing themselves to new items and often on a daily basis. This sub-group has some of the characteristics of overspending.

One of the classic examples of this addictive behavior was an 80 year old man from western Tennessee. He had been collecting "junk" for over 40 years and couldn't stop. He had everything from a stuffed alligator to a 40' windmill. This man would get up at midnight to head out for an auction to add to his collection which he stored on an acre of land. It seems that his excitement and enthusiasm for buying and collecting quickly took over his original intention to operate a small store. "I feel like I have a tiger by the tail," he laments. "I've got boxes and boxes and boxes that I haven't had the time to look through yet." And even though he keeps saying he's going to stop buying, every time a pickup pulls into his place with a load of new items, he winds up with even more.

In this country with a 322,000,000 population there are almost half that many cats and dogs. 65% of US households have one or more pets.

If you hoard or collect pets, when by the sheer numbers alone (I had one client with 45 cats), causes them harm by lack of food, inadequate shelter or cleanliness, too little emotional support, or inadequate healthcare, or when this hoarding harms you by costing too much for food, grooming, flea and worm medication, anxiety and depression, decreased socialization with neighbors and family, inability to leave them for other pursuits, and you refuse to re-home some or all of your pets, this is an addiction. You may see this as a benevolent act of love for your pets, but in actuality you're looking for unconditional love which you haven't gotten from humans and an attempt to feel better about your self and bolster your low self-esteem.

The same treatment program works for all of the addictive behaviors we have mentioned. Since addiction is a spiritual disease, it is my goal to teach you how to spiritually arrest and cure this addictive process in your life. Through enhanced self-awareness and spiritual insight, any and all of these behaviors can be treated and eliminated. These temporary human conditions can be cured and eliminated when you finally understand and learn to appreciate your destiny and your value as a person and as a child of God.

Chapter Fifteen How God Revealed His Plan For Curing Addiction

In order for you to be able to believe that you can get well from addiction I am now going to tell you my story. Every word of this story is true, provable, and documentable, but I don't want my personal drama to take away from God's story and so in this final edition I have abridged the longer version which you can find in a previous edition.

This addiction treatment program was very important and special to God. He provided all the things needed in order to get this message out to the world. This is not my program. It is God's plan and that is why it always works. God never makes mistakes.

In the 80's I opened a single physician outpatient family practice in Knoxville Tennessee. It quickly became evident that many of my new patients were addicted to mood altering medications...Valium in particular...that had been prescribed by their previous doctors.

At the time, the government was making a lot of noise about doctors over prescribing medications and several physicians in my community had been warned. The government began checking all the pharmacies and within a year DEA and FBI agents considered me a person of interest. I was in the middle of a clinical study into Valium addiction and it was generating large numbers of prescriptions.

The government started harassing my patients and employees, trying to find something I was doing wrong in respect to my prescribing Valium. However they never came to me to ask directly why I was writing a large number of prescriptions for that particular drug. They also tried to find fraud in my medicare billing system. They took all my medical files downtown and had people going through them trying to find something illegal. Still, after a year of continuous investigation, they had found no evidence of wrong doing.

During this time, I had a problem with one of my employees who was also the clinic manager. I discovered she was stealing drugs from the pharmacy for resale on the street. When I had my attorney draw up a legal document where she had to admit her guilt, she became angry. I had done this to try to control her behavior...in retrospect, a big mistake. This was an example of my own codependency/control addiction. Knowing she could get in serious trouble if I reported her stealing from our pharmacy, she started collaborating with the FBI to protect herself from her illegal activities. She wore a "wire" and arranged numerous "discussions" with me regarding the ongoing FBI-DEA investigation.

She told me she would get the government investigation stopped (but wouldn't say how) if I would put $30,000 into a fund for her kids' college educations. I agreed (she was very convincing as she was a sociopath, but I would not give her the money directly. I thought I was delivering the money to her investment broker, but he turned out to be an FBI agent. The government was trying to entrap me into a crime of attempted bribery of a government agent. Like a sheep to slaughter, I stepped into their well laid trap.

I found myself in a staged trial that smeared my reputation all over the newspapers, with a judge who would not allow my defense team to put on a witness witness with four doctoral degrees who could interpret the "wire" tapes and vindicate me. My defense team in preparation for the federal trial had two mock trials. In both of these trials I was found not guilty, but in the federal trial I was found guilty.

In a typical intimidation senario, many months later, federal prosecutors threatened me with a longer sentence and the possibility of involving my elderly parents if I did not capitulate and plead guilty to at least one count of over-prescribing Valium. Backed into this impossible legal corner and depleted of all assets to fight, I picked a likely patient and completed the statement they wanted, even though I had done nothing wrong.

When my experience with the federal government was over, I had a private investigator find the patient that the government forced me to lie about and she signed a document stating that she had only gotten the normal amount of Valium for the two months I was treating her.

In November 1990, I found myself in a holding cell which was dark 23 hours a day. This was sheer torture, and I felt completely isolated, unloved, and violated. The first weeks were filled with strong emotions as I prayed and tried to figure out why I was there. I felt incredibly violated for trusting in a system that did not do the right thing.

I began to really question my life and cried out to God to let me know why I was stuck in this dark hole. God did not take long in giving me the answer. In a dream vision, He told me, "You possess the knowledge and experience to write a book that I want written about addiction. If you choose to accept this mission, I will protect you while you are in prison. I will provide all the materials needed to write the book and the money to publish it. Finally, you will be released when the book is published."

When God wants to work in your life, He often gives you a dream...about yourself, about what he wants you to do, about how he's going to use your life to impact the world.

There is a rich history in the Bible of God giving His children dreams for their lives. God gave Noah the dream of building an ark. He gave Abraham the dream of being the father of a great nation. God gave Joseph the dream of being a leader that would save his people. He gave Nehemiah the dream of building the wall around Jerusalem.

In the history of the Bible the foremost way that men knew that God had spoken to them was through prophecy (to predict or reveal through written or spoken words divine inspiration). If a prophecy that was attributed to God later came true it was assumed that it came from God. The more unlikely the prophesy the more the believablity that it had indeed come from God.

Everyone I shared this prophecy with was convinced that I had lost my mind. They labeled it "Jail House Religion." I on the other hand believed that God's promise to me was real and I set about writing the book.

In that instant that I accepted my mission I was spiritually transformed. I was born again. I looked around me and saw only my Bible and a few meager personal belongings, yet I felt a happiness in my heart that I had never felt before.

The prison system is not conducive to creative endeavors. Often napkins became my notepaper and with the lights off 23 hours a day I was forced to go to the end of the cage to get enough light to write. Eventually I was transferred to another facility that had better arrangements, and **the entire time God kept me safe from harm fulfilling the first prophecy.**

He produced the funds ($5,000) to publish the book by way of a gift from a fellow prisoner fulfilling the second prophecy.

When I received a copy of the finished book in the mail, I remembered God's promise to me that I would be released when the book was completed. And here's the fantastic fulfillment of the third part of the prophecy. **Within 40 hours of receiving the book, a guard came to my cell and announced that I was going home, fulfilling the third prophecy!** My sentence was 33 months, but I had only served 24 months at that point. Remember there is no parole in the federal system.

The chance of those three events happening by coincidence would be much smaller than the chance of winning the lottery. No this was no coincidence. This was a fulfilled promise of God. Yes, this is God's plan not mine. I am merely the messenger. And this is why this addiction treatment program always works. It works because it's God's plan and God never makes mistakes.

Chapter Sixteen Treatment and Recovery

As I previously explained the reason this treatment plan always works is that the plan came from God, and God doesn't make mistakes.

Jesus said to them, "You are truly my disciples if you live as I tell you to, and you will know the truth, and the truth will set you free." John 8:31, 32 TLB

"He sent me to heal the broken hearted and to announce that captives shall be released and the blind shall see, that the downtrodden shall be freed from their oppressors, and that God is ready to give blessings to all who come to Him." Luke 4:18 TLB

The first requirement is wanting to get well.

Remember the story of the healing at the pool in Bethesda. One of the men lying there had been sick for thirty-eight years. When Jesus saw him and knew how long he had been ill, He asked him, "Would you like to get well?" Jesus told him, "Stand up, roll up your sleeping mat and go home!" John 5: 5-6, 8 TLB

The second requirement for success is belief and faith that the program will work. To be 100% effective, the treatment plan must be accepted completely.

Your beliefs influence your behavior. We always act according to our beliefs, even when those ideas are false. For instance, as a child, if you believed a shadow in your bedroom at night was a monster, your body would react in fear (adrenaline and jitters) even though it wasn't true. That's why it's so important to make sure you are operating on true information! Your beliefs about yourself, about life, and about God will influence your actions and what happens to you in life.

2000 years ago a woman came to Jesus with the faith that if she touched him the bleeding that she had for 12 years would stop and she would be healed. Having accomplished this miracle, Jesus said,

"Daughter....Your faith has healed you. Go in peace." Luke 8:48 TLB

Faith can accomplish what the world dismisses as impossible. "I tell you the truth, if you have the faith as small as a mustard seed, you can say to this mountain, 'move from here to there' and it will move. Nothing will be impossible for you." Matthew 17:21 NIV

Do miracles happen today just like they did 2000 years ago? Can prayer and faith today still create the environment for a healing miracle?

Read the story of Dorene Poe: "I had a stroke on September 27 of 2007. I was in Mission hospital in Asheville for six days. Ruth stayed with me until my family came up from Leesburg, Florida. Pastor Peoples was there for me even though I wasn't there for myself. It took days before I could speak and I took personal credit for the recovery. It was just me, me, me. I stayed at my sister's house for four months."

Then on December 27 of 2009, "I had another episode which might have been a seizure. At the hospital I had a second seizure in front of a neurologist. He said it was a classic case of seizure coming from my left frontal lobe. Using brain scans diagnosed it as an astrocytoma (a malignant brain tumor).

I had brain surgery scheduled for January 20. On the Sunday before I was scheduled for surgery friends were praying for me. My daughter held one hand and Paula held the other. I felt a hot feeling in my head in the area where I had my stroke. I said, Something just happened to me. [It was God healing me].

I had my surgery and the surgeon could not find the tumor. He told me that he had done four thousand of these surgeries and this is the first time that he had made a misdiagnosis like this. So I told him what had

happened to me....that God had taken care of it!"

The third requirement is working the treatment program, daily and continually.

If these three conditions are met, one cannot fail to be completely cured. Failure is not a possibility. The three choices however, rest with the individual.

Once upon a time a man heard it raining outside. Over the next few hours, it continued to rain. It rained and it rained and it rained. The man was fearful because it had flooded in his neighborhood before. And so he climbed out on the roof. The water kept coming up and up and up. He was a religious man and prayed to God for God to save him.

A big log floated by the house. The man was scared to jump off the roof and hang on to the log, so he continued to sit right where he was waiting for God to save him.

Next a dingy came by. The problem here was that all the seats were taken, and he would have to hold onto the side. He decided to wait on God.

Finally, a helicopter came by close to the roof with a rope hanging down. The pilot yelled for him to grab the rope, but he was afraid that he would slip off the rope and drown so he waited on God.

The water continued to rise and swept him off the roof into the churning water. He drowned and went to heaven. When he saw God he said, "I prayed and prayed to you to save me."

God replied, "I sent you a log, a boat, and a helicopter." Regardless of the fact that you want to get well, like the man who wanted to get off the roof, and regardless of the fact that you have plenty of faith and belief, if you don't follow your desire and belief with action, you will still drown. You will still fail to get well.

Some will completely reject the concept. Some will only partially accept it or only partially work the plan. Both will fail to be cured. They may abstain from their current addictive behavior, but the disease is active waiting for an opportunity to recur.

Generally the difference between those who make the commitment and are successful and those who are not successful depends on whether their lives have become too unmanageable...whether the addictions have caused them so much loss that they are willing to do anything to stop the pain and suffering.

Many people attend recovery programs but are not committed. Just as other programs will fail if there is no commitment on the individual's part, so will this program. However, since this program is always effective with sufficient belief and continued work, one can accurately gauge the sincerity of the individual based on the results of treatment.

Complete recovery is the goal we are interested in. It is our ultimate objective. The (revised) twelve steps can be a significant force in reaching that goal. Once we understand what the twelve steps mean, they can be followed individually through personal inner work, working with friends, associates, or counselors, or in the group meeting experience.

Walking a spiritual path is the answer for recovery, but how this is done is the individual's choice. This choice is made after sufficient prayer and meditation has resulted in understanding. Whatever you feel works best for you is in fact, the best plan. After you have recovered, you will feel differently from the way you felt before. You will act differently. You will think differently, because you will be a new, different person.

In Stan Katz's book, The "Co-dependency Conspiracy," he lists ten points that signify recovery. I would like to share them with you. You are recovered (cured) when:

YOU NO LONGER ENGAGE IN THE PROBLEM BEHAVIOR.

YOU NO LONGER CRAVE THE PROBLEM BEHAVIOR.

Recovery requires satisfying the hidden needs causing the craving. The hidden needs are, of course, improvement of self-esteem and the need for a better developed understanding of "the truth of life" (the four questions). Once this hidden agenda is taken care of, the old person is no more. The new person, who used to be addicted to alcohol, for the purpose of an example, is able to take that drink with dinner without the fear of falling back into the trap of alcohol abuse.

YOUR THOUGHTS AND CONVERSATIONS ARE NO LONGER DOMINATED BY THE SAME RECURRENT PROBLEMS.

At this point you do not feel the need to continue to go to self-help groups as before. Your thoughts and attention can now focus on other pursuits, goals, and activities.

YOU ARE NOT HOOKED ON SUBSTITUTE ADDICTIONS.

Some addictions are no doubt healthier than others, but to substitute coffee and 12-step meetings for cocaine use is not recovery. Any addiction will prevent your spiritual growth, development, and ultimate recovery.

YOU NO LONGER BLAME YOUR PAST MISTAKES FOR CURRENT FRUSTRATIONS, AND DISAPPOINTMENTS.

It is important for a recovered person not to use past addictive behaviors as an excuse for current problems. Instead one needs to face today's problems directly.

YOU NO LONGER NEED PROBLEMS TO MAKE YOU FEEL SPECIAL OR UNIQUE.

With recovery, your self-esteem has increased to the point that you don't need to use your disease as a badge of honor to make yourself feel special or to get attention. You feel special because your inner work has caused you to love yourself and to accept yourself for the valuable person you really are.

YOUR SOCIAL LIFE NO LONGER REVOLVES AROUND YOUR PROBLEMS.

Healthy, growing relationships are not based on disease associations, but on vital, dynamic ones which result in new perspectives and challenges.

YOU HAVE THE TOOLS AND AWARENESS TO PREVENT OTHER PROBLEMS FROM OVERTAKING YOUR LIFE.

When fully recovered, you are able to realistically identify, confront, and deal effectively with new problems as they develop. When they are beyond your ability to solve them, you do not have difficulty seeking outside help.

YOUR LIFE IS IN BALANCE.

The scale is not tipped too far in either direction. Your daily existence is now manageable and happy. You have peace of mind and success.

YOU NO LONGER VIEW LIFE EXCLUSIVELY IN TERMS OF "ONE DAY AT A TIME", BUT TAKE THINGS AS THEY COME, EMBRACING THE LONGER VIEW OF THE FUTURE.

Initially it was necessary to view life in small blocks of time to focus on attainable goals. Recovered, you can live in the present looking forward to all of life's possibilities.

Let's get started with your personal recovery right now! Here are the treatment's plan five steps:

STEP ONE: Education

STEP TWO: Creativity

STEP THREE: Physical Fitness

STEP FOUR: Forgiveness - Helping Others

STEP FIVE: Spiritual Development

Each step will be discussed separately and a specific plan will be developed by you to satisfy each step. How you accomplish each step

is your decision, but **each step must be worked on continually to affect a cure.** Your individual plan should be noted on the calendar.

Freedom from Addiction Workshop Calendar																														
Day of Week																															
Day of the month	1	2	3	4	5	6	7	8	9	10	11	12	13	14	15	16	17	18	19	20	21	22	23	24	25	26	27	28	29	30	31
Step 1																															
Step 2																															
Step 3																															
Step 4A																															
Step 4B																															
Step 5A																															
Step 5B																															
Step 5C																															
Step 5D																															
Step 5E																															
Step 5F																															
My Goals:																															
1																															
2																															
3																															
4																															
5																															

Step One: Education

This is the first step of the treatment program. There are many possibilities for education. You can go back to school at whatever level you find yourself. School could be academic or vocational. It could entail active classroom participation, or be by the internet or mail correspondence. Education might entail reading or learning through audio or video formats or by reading books.

Step One: Education. I will (describe the educational plans you have) _____ I will do this on a _____ (describe the frequency) basis.

Step Two: Creativity

Marion Woodman once said that if we fail to nourish our souls, they wither, and without soul, life ceases to have meaning. Creativity is one of the things that makes life worth living.

Expressing yourself as the unique, valuable person you really are is necessary to affect a cure from your disease. Creativity improves and reinforces your self-esteem. There are any number of ways an individual can express his or her creativity.

Do you sing, dance, paint, invent, write, play an instrument, restore automobiles, make gourmet meals, or work with crafts? It makes no difference how you express yourself as long as it is something you like

to do and something you feel good about doing. **From this day forward, you must, in order to recover, be actively engaged in some type of creative pursuit.** The frequency of the activity and the amount of time spent on it will obviously vary for each individual. Just be sure you keep at it. Of course you can change the creative pursuit from time to time as you wish.

Step Two Creativity. I will start _____ (describe the type of creative activity). I will do this activity on a _____ (describe the frequency you will do it) basis.

Step Three: Physical Fitness

Honor God with your body.1 Corinthians 6:20 . Our bodies were made for activity. In Bible times they didn't have to exercise because they walked everywhere they went. They did physical work. But most of us have sedentary lives and we drive everywhere. Yet you really only have two choices in life: fatigue or fitness. Fitness involves regular exercise. Just as improving the mind and developing one's creativity will improve self-esteem, so does improving the physical body.

There are countless ways to do this, everything from weight lifting to jazzercise. Any plan you can do on a regular continuing basis is satisfactory. All that is required is to pick a program you like and stick to it! I recommend starting with a walking program unless you have something you like better. Get a comfortable pair of sneakers and find a walking route that the round trip will take you 30 minutes to complete. Plan to walk everyday for this period of time unless you are prevented by illness, emergency, or the weather. On your calendar mark the number of minutes you walk every day in red. Try your best not to go a day without some amount of time being recorded. If you average 3.5 miles per hour and walk an hour daily you are walking 25 miles a week and burning enough extra calories to lose 1.1 pounds per week just from this exercise alone.

Walking is also a good time to meditate and pray, but if you don't want to "double up" at this time, you might consider a "walkman" with headphones. This makes the time go faster.

In addition to the other benefits, walking is a good method of improving your cardiovascular health and increasing your life span.

Step Three-Physical Fitness. Starting today, I will _____ _____ describe the type of exercise you will do). I will do this for _____ minutes on a _____ basis (record the frequency).

Step Four: Forgiveness - Helping Others

Forgiveness seems to be the spiritual key needed to continue the spiritual journey which ultimately results in healing and curing your disease. Jesus taught a basic Christian principal which can be found in the Lord's Prayer: *Forgive Others And You Will Be Forgiven.*

Your forgiveness is based on first forgiving others, all the others in the world who have ever hurt you. Each of us have been hurt by being rejected, abandoned, humiliated, disappointed, betrayed, deceived, or abused and all these hurts lower our self-esteem.

In addition to its effect on our addictive behaviors, the effects of lack of forgiveness can be seen in physical symptoms (like colitis, ulcers, and high blood pressure), psychological and psychiatric symptoms, and all sorts of relationship problems.

Forgiveness is not about forgetting, condoning, absolving, self-sacrificing, or something that is done for someone else's benefit. Forgiving is done to heal ourselves and set us free. The inner peace we seek can never be found in trying to change other people who have hurt us. It can only be found as we change ourselves.

Many books have been written on how to forgive. Seminars have been given to teach this necessary act. These are valuable tools, but ultimately the basis for success is the sincere desire, freely given, to release hate, anger, and other self-destructive negative emotions against all of humanity and against ourselves.

As you grew and developed, you were hurt by what you didn't get but desperately needed: love, closeness, safety, affection, attention, guidance, encouragement, and validation of self-worth. All the alcohol, drugs, food, work, sex, or spending sprees you could engage in over a lifetime can not replace what you did not get from your parents, spouses, lovers, friends, or anyone else who hurt you.

Unconditional love is the healing power behind forgiveness, and self love provides the basis for the desire to forgive and to heal. Only a free person with a good self concept can choose to live with an uneven score or an unsettled account. **Until we feel good enough about ourselves to forgive others, we will never be able to forgive ourselves.** It is this ability to forgive ourselves that allows us to wash away the guilt and shame that has been feeding our compulsions and addictions for so long.

Step 4A—Forgiveness. Make a list of everyone who has ever hurt you and briefly review in your mind what the hurt(s) were. Now simply affirm: *I now forgive everyone who has ever hurt me. I forgive myself for all my prior mistakes and accept God's forgiveness also.*

Reaffirm this thought three times a day for at least 60 days and thereafter whenever you feel negative emotions resulting from lack of forgiveness. Anytime in the future, when thoughts of anger, hate, revenge, or resentment come to you, repeat the affirmation above until the thoughts are gone.

Step 4B - Help Others. The second part of this step is to help another person at least once a day without being motivated to get something in return. Being of service to others raises your self-esteem immeasurably. On your calendar, there are blanks along the bottom to record what you did each day to help another. Review the list at the end of each month.

The degree and extent that you help others is not the most important aspect of accomplishing this step. Some days you may do more than other days. The most important thing is to consistently help others and to be in the right mental attitude to be looking around for good you can do for another person.

Step Five--Spiritual Development

One's spiritual development is the most important reason for our creation. In it is answered the quest for immortality and eternal survival. Since your soul doesn't die, it doesn't matter how fast this development is accomplished, for you have forever to fully accomplish it. I often tell people, "It doesn't matter how fast you walk, but rather that you just keep walking."

What does matter in terms of this life is that you understand your relationship to God, other people, and the world in general, and that with this understanding you develop it and nurture it as you live your life. **Your goal in this life is to discover God's plan for your life (your mission/destiny) and to carry it out.**

With the proper understanding of the true nature of your being, which is the essence of metaphysical philosophy and embodied in the four questions, you will cure your disease. With this understanding you can be at peace with yourself and the world and become successful beyond your wildest dreams.

This fifth step is sub-divided into six parts. They are:

5A—Discovering Your Mission

5B—The Twelve Step Program

5C–Affirmation/Prayer

5D–Meditation

5E–Changing Associations

5F–Organized Religion/Bible Study

5A–Discovering Your Mission

The third question, "*What am I doing here?*" is extremely important as it directly relates to the most self-esteem enhancing single understanding that a person can have. Since one cannot focus on two different ideas of the same time, **if one is focused on their mission or purpose in life, they will not be focusing on their addictive behaviors.**

The easiest way to find out what is your mission or purpose in life is to pray:

"If I had no limitations in life, neither financial, educational, intelligence, nor any other kind, and I was not influenced by what other's thought (not husband, not wife. not family. not friends, not business associates), what would I do with my life that on ending would be the best I could have done to unconditionally love and help others?"

and through meditation, wait on the answer. When the answer arrives, drop your fishing nets just as the disciples did 2000 years ago and pursue your mission and destiny. In this way your problem with addictions will be solved.

5B—The 12 Step Program.

Most people who attend twelve step meetings feel that they are never actually cured. They must "keep coming back" to the meetings in order to abstain from their addiction of choice. They feel that one use or "slip" will propel them down the road to full blown uncontrolled addictive behavior.

The twelve steps is a spiritual program. It requires one to recognize that a problem exists that the individual cannot control. One must believe in a "higher power" and turn one's will and life over to that "higher power" to direct the individual. One must believe that by doing so, the problem (addictive behavior) can be resolved. One must develop personal integrity and work on getting rid of character defects. One must be willing, and as much as possible, make amends to all people the individual has harmed. There is a requirement to pray and meditate for God's guidance. And there is also a directive to spread the message and practice the 12 step principles in day-to-day living.

I have revised the original twelve steps to incorporate a step for forgiveness. By combining the original step six and seven, which go well together, a place for a forgiveness step is created. The book I wrote to explain this is: *The 12 Steps: A Recovery Program Explained And Revised. This book is currently out of print.*

Imagine having a mountain summit as your goal and after many days of successful climbing, stopping at a crevice just 100 yards from the top: 99% successful but not quite there. At the top is a flat, safe area where one cannot fall. One hundred yards from the top, you are still on the wall, exposed to danger, with the chance to slip.

What makes the difference in your final position? It is the healing power of forgiveness. Through forgiveness one is able to cross the crevice for the final climb to ultimate success and safety. When you are able to sincerely, and in truth, forgive everyone who has ever hurt you, then and only then, will you be able to accept God's forgiveness and to forgive yourself too.

Only then will the self depreciating feelings of guilt and shame and past mistakes disappear and self-esteem be fully restored. No complete cure of the disease is possible until this happens.

You can work with a mentor. You can attend twelve step meetings where the program is discussed. You can also go straight to God through prayer.

Step 5B- The 12 step program. I will _____ _____ (describe how you plan to learn and practice the 12 steps in order to "work" the program. I will do this on a _____ (describe the frequency basis).

Step 5C—Affirmations/Prayer

To affirm is "to declare or maintain to be true." An affirmation is the declaration itself, either verbalized or merely thought. A prayer is the expression of thoughts, hopes, or needs to God. Therefore an affirmation directed towards God is a prayer. If a prayer is infused with belief, and if the belief is strong enough, it is answered. Go to chapter 17 to get a fuller description of affirmations.

Prayers can be good or bad, and if we believe in them they are answered. This is one of the reasons it is better to have good thoughts coming from you than destructive, bad thoughts.

Some use prayer as merely a spasmodic cry out of an occasional crisis. This makes prayer utterly selfish. Some see prayer as an obligation, not the supreme privilege it really is: a chance to develop a friendship with God. Some pray impatiently, fast and fretful, and then when immediate results don't come, they give up and quit. But for those who pray habitually, continuously, not seeking God's gifts as much as his companionship and wisdom, those lucky individuals gain the full benefit of the experience.

Prayer converts the mere idea of God as existing, into a dynamic helpful presence in one's life. Many see prayer as a form....like "saying prayers." And yet the highest form of prayer we are told, is continuous. We obviously cannot say formalized prayers continuously and don't need to. In fact, the Bible warns against vain repetition in prayers.

When prayer becomes a conscious fellowship with God, who is seen as our father who cares and wants the best for us in every way, the individual who is praying then begins to realize and accept the fact that God has a personal interest in him or her and can and will use His power on behalf of the individual. This dramatically improves one's self-esteem.

Step 5D—Meditation

Over the years I have learned that meditation is one of the six critical areas of spiritual discipline that is necessary to recover from the disease of addiction. Through meditation, an individual receives incoming communication from God. We may pray continuously, but to obtain wisdom, which is what God has to offer us, we must set aside time to listen for His guidance. God rarely speaks in sounds we can hear. Our communication usually comes in extrasensory, intuitive form. When we ask and believe, we receive, but we must prepare ourselves for the answer. The philosophy and ideas in this book did not originate with me. They came unexpectedly in a dream, one cold winter night in late November, 1990, in answer to a prayer for understanding..... "What am I doing here?" Receiving insight during dreams is wonderful. It requires no effort except for writing it down before one falls back to sleep. But this serendipitous form of receiving guidance is also somewhat lazy. If you accept M. Scott Peck's definition of love as "the degree one is willing to extend oneself for spiritual development," you can see that in truly loving oneself, effort is required. Love then becomes the evolutionary force behind spiritual development for the individual and for the world.

How does one meditate? Book after book has been written on this topic, but let me share with you one way of getting in the proper plane for effective meditation. Meditation needs to be done when you can divorce yourself from what's going on in the world for the moment. You can use a progressive muscle relaxation technique followed by a breathing control technique to accomplish this.

First lie or sit down in a comfortable place away from as many distractions as possible. Start by contracting the muscles of the feet, then the lower legs, then the upper legs, the stomach, the shoulders, the arms, the neck, and the face in that order, and hold on to the muscle contraction for a count of five. Release. Contract all the muscles in your body for a count of five. Release. Repeat the process once or twice until you can feel the relaxation.

Now on a count of four breathe in. Hold the breath for a count of four. Breathe out for a count of four. Do this for a minute or two. You should now be in a meditative state of mind and responsive to incoming messages from the supraconsciousness (God).

Another method many people use is to simply walk alone (without music or any other interruption). This also seems very effective as a meditation technique. Every discipline requires continuity of effort. In order to reverse the human characteristics of laziness, one needs motivation and reminders. Try keeping a diary and each day record the number of minutes you spend meditating. **Make time for daily meditation even if it's just ten minutes.**

Remember your priorities. You want to get better. Briefly state the guidance you seek (in the form of a prayer) and write it down. Record your intuitive feelings at the end of the session. Do this daily. From time to time go back and review your journal. You'll be surprised with the insights that it reveals and how those insights develop in your life.

Step 5D—Meditation.

I will meditate_____ minutes a day. I plan to do this _____

_____ (describe the time of day).

Step 5E—Changing Associations

It would, I suppose, be nice if we didn't have to critically evaluate our associates and associations and how they effect our disease process. Of course this is the easy way out and practically anything that is easy, turns out not to be very valuable. In order to accomplish this step, one must look at all those people and associations which negatively impact on our getting well. This may include dropping some old "friends." It may entail changing a job. It might go so far as getting a divorce, or only seeing one's parents on an occasional basis. Only you can determine what is necessary for you to get well. But remember you must look after yourself first. One can never love another until one loves and values himself or herself first.

I once knew a seven year old named Timmy who wanted very badly to buy his daddy a card for his birthday. But on Timmy's meager allowance his money never seemed to accumulate fast enough, especially since Timmy would buy ice cream everyday when the ice cream man came around.

Timmy was tempted daily to spend his money for pleasure rather than save it for a higher purpose. One day Timmy was overheard praying out loud, "God, give me strength to run away when I hear the ice cream man coming." Timmy instinctively grasped this concept at an early age. If you want to overcome addiction, stay as far away from the attachment(s) as you possibly can.

Step 5E—Changing Associations.

I will complete this step by_____
_____ (describe what you must do to satisfy the requirements of this is step). In this way I will help cure my disease.

Step 5F—Organized Religion--Bible--Inspirational Reading

This part of the program of spiritual development can be accomplished by either participating in organized religious services, by reading the Bible, or by reading inspirational materials. Some people, for a number of reasons, do not feel comfortable "going to church," and it is not necessary to do so. One may find that spiritual development comes faster by reading scripture, or reading inspirational material and trying to understand it in terms of general principles (instead of literal word for word translation).

Chapter Seventeen Affirmations

Each thought and word you speak is an affirmation. All of our self talk, or internal dialogue, is a constant flow of affirmations. Our brain makes words that get repeated over and over time part of our identity, whether they are positive or negative, inherently true or false. My intention then is to feed ourselves with whatever affirmations will create the shift in mindset that supports our goals and builds a healthy picture of our identity.

To affirm is "to declare or maintain to be true." An affirmation is the declaration itself, either verbalized or merely thought. A prayer is the expression of thoughts, hopes, or needs to God. Therefore an affirmation directed towards God is a prayer. If a prayer is infused with belief, and if the belief is strong enough, it is answered, sometimes yes, sometimes no, and sometimes you will have to wait.

Prayers can be good or bad, and if we believe in them they are answered. This is one of the reasons it is better to have good thoughts coming from you than destructive, bad thoughts.

Some use prayer as merely a spasmodic cry out of an occasional crisis. This makes prayer utterly selfish. Some see prayer as an obligation, not the supreme privilege it really is: a chance to develop a friendship with God. Some pray impatiently, fast and fretful, and then when immediate results don't come, they give up and quit. But for those who pray habitually, continuously, not seeking God's gifts as much as his companionship and wisdom, those lucky individuals gain the full benefit of the experience. Prayer converts the mere idea of God as existing, into a dynamic helpful presence in one's life.

Many see prayer as a form...like "saying prayers." And yet the highest form of prayer we are told, is continuous. We obviously cannot say formalized prayers continuously and don't need to. In fact, the Bible warns against vain repetition in prayers. When prayer becomes a conscious fellowship with God, who is seen as our father who cares and wants the best for us in every way, the individual who is praying then begins to realize and accept the fact that God has a personal interest in him or her and can and will use His power on behalf of the individual. This dramatically improves one's self-esteem. Low self-esteem is the underlying cause of all of the addictive behaviors.

Is there any wonder then that the power capable of creating not only this world, but also the universe, is capable of curing our problems with addiction?

The power is there and God wants to help us heal. Initially all that is required is that we truly believe and ask for the help. By truly believing in the concept of God, His relationship to us, and our relationship to the rest of the world, we develop the attitude of willingness to do God's will whatever that might be. The test of true prayer is putting ourselves at God's disposal. Prayer cannot change God's purpose, but prayer can release it. Prayer gives God the opportunity to do what His wisdom and love wants done.

One of the fundamental tools in the treatment program is using affirmations to increase your self image and self-esteem. You can hand pick the affirmations from this book to "custom design" the type of person you want to become or the thoughts you want to believe in. Or using the examples found in this book you can write your own affirmations. This is especially important for goal affirmations which are different for each of us.

"As a person thinks in the depths of his heart, that is the way he really is." Proverbs 23:7 This means that whatever concept your subconscious mind holds of you, that in truth, is the real you.

We can change ourselves by affirmations. The process is speeded up by creative visualization (which essentially is creating an imaginary mental picture of the situation or goal you are affirming). You must believe that what you ask for is already the case and that you are now waiting on delivery.

Consciousness is present day reality as you know it. It contains your thoughts, feelings, and emotions. You have freedom of choice on this level. You relate directly to the world or "outer experience" using your five conscious senses. Consciousness accounts for one third of your mind.

The second third of your mind is subconsciousness. It is not readily accessible to your five senses. It accepts the thoughts, feelings, and emotions dumped into it by the conscious mind. You could look at it as a warehouse for your thoughts. The function of this part of your mind is not to question, but merely to accept the ideas given to it, and then to work continuously to bring these ideas into reality. The subconscious works with the "outer experience" on a level beyond our five senses to make this happen. Affirmations are stored in the subconscious mind.

The third part of the mind is the supraconsciousness or GOD within us. It is perfect wisdom, understanding, conscience, guidance, and knowledge. This part of the mind only knows good and only perfect truth can come from it. The supraconsciouness is tapped by prayer and meditation. Its resources come to the conscious mind through intuition and extrasensory perception. This part of the mind also relates to the world or "outer experience", and can from time to time directly influence the world when it is for the fulfillment of GOD's plan for the individual.

These three parts of the mind form the "inner experience" and determine what happens in our lives. The power of positive affirmation or prayer cannot be denied. Proof is all around us. You can seldom open a newspaper without reading about some "miracle" that has happened somewhere to someone. Miracles are however, not that unusual for people who are spiritually inclined. Miracles are merely the answers to prayers, and they are delivered many times daily in some degree or another to those who claim them.

"For verily I say until you, that whosoever shall say unto this mountain, be thou removed and be thou cast into the sea; and shall believe that these things which he saith shall come to pass, he shall have whatsoever he saith. Therefore I say unto you, what things soever ye desire when ye pray, believe that you receive them, and ye shall have them." Mark 11:23-24.

This is the highest authority that affirmations (prayers) are valid and will give you what you seek. This teaching by Jesus helps form the spiritual basis for success of the treatment program.

One can divide affirmations into three groups: those for development of spiritualization and self-esteem, those for healing, and those for goal development.

There has been considerable thought on how long it takes to make a new affirmation part of one's subconsciousness. The minimum is probably 60 days. Your affirmations should be said on arising, at least once during the day, (individual ones more frequently if you are experiencing a particular problem), and at night just before retiring.

I recommend you select no more than 5 affirmations initially, some from each of the three groups, and to use them as outlined for 60 days. At that time change some of them for others in the group. In this way you will have something new to think about every eight weeks. If your goal affirmations have not been reached, keep them or modify them. Some of the other affirmations may be so necessary for your spiritual development that you will want to leave them in continuously.

My favorite affirmation is: **I am the one. This is the place. Now is the time. His hand is upon me.**

What it comes down to is this: first we have a thought. The thought is expressed to God as a prayer. During quiet meditation God responds with guidance and imparts His wisdom. We then act on that direction and carry it out. In this way we always obtain the absolute best result and we are healed from our disease.

I wish that I could tell you that once you have finished eight weeks of therapy you would always be cured of your disease and nothing more had to be done.

Unfortunately, that is not the case, for this is a life long journey. **A spiritual treatment is the only truly effective treatment and it requires daily attention forever.** It requires you to become a new and different person from the one you were before. Some refer to this as becoming "born again." This new person no longer has a problem with all the addictive behaviors because there is no need, or even desire, for them again.

The pay-off for this effort, however, is that you will be successful beyond your wildest dreams. You will have happiness, joy, contentment, fulfillment, satisfaction, ultimate security, and peace of mind. In this sense you will be richer than kings with a type of wealth that can never be taken from you. All your needs will be met as you pray for what you need and continue your journey down your spiritual path.

Now here is a list of over 200 affirmations to get you started:

The choices I make will often affect my family line for generations to come. My children and grandchildren have enough to overcome without having to deal with my negative baggage.

I live my life in such a way that I cause others to win.

Remember the story of Abraham and Sarah in the Bible. If you will give up on Ishmael, Isaac will show up.

When you go through some dark times, perhaps they are there to toughen you up. Now don't complain. There are blessings that can come out of them. Faith is believing that the dark times are there for your good.

God is not limited by the facts. Choose faith in spite of them.

If you want to be a rainmaker spend more time sending up vapor to praise God. This is the fastest way to fill your cloud.

Freedom from addiction begins in my mind. I don't have to be chained forever.

I was created to be who I was destined to be. I am God's masterpiece and most prized possession. I am extremely valuable!

A painting's value doesn't come so much for what it looks like, but rather who the painter was.

I am heavy with God's favor and I expect it.

God's mercy is greater than my worst mistake. I am forgiven! God will bless me in spite of my history.

My body, mind, and spirit are in harmony with myself, God, and the world. I exercise, eat properly, and maintain a positive mental attitude every day.

I have a sense of calm within me that permeates every cell of my body.

During quiet prayer and meditation I acknowledge God's presence within me. Where I am, there is God also. We are never separated, for daily we walk hand in hand.

Today I let go and let God. By doing so I became a productive individual who is able to reach my highest destiny and find ultimate happiness and satisfaction in life.

I am important and needed. I have a great gift to give to the world simply by being myself and following God's will and plan for my life.

I rely on God for Justice. No longer do I expect justice from myself, society, or government. I now understand that judgments can only be made on absolute truth and only God is capable of that complete understanding.

Today I completely forgive myself and others for past errors and mistakes. I release guilt, shame, and resentment. As negative feelings leave, they are replaced by peace, joy, and contentment.

As I develop spiritually, I go from possessing people and things to loving people. I do not need to possess either people or things. Reducing my inventory gives me serenity and peace of mind.

When I am wrong I promptly admit it, for by humility I can continue my spiritual growth.

Today I share what I have with others. I renounce hoarding, over possessing, and gluttony. I let go of my greedy and selfish ways. My mind works with self-confidence and faith. I put doubt aside. I believe in myself and persist in my efforts. I can not fail.

Some people don't mean what they say. Some people don't say what they mean. Some lie. I tell the truth and am honest, not only with others but also with myself.

I am committed to personal integrity because I want spiritual growth. To continue even small dishonest behaviors stops me dead in my spiritual tracts.

I do not wear a mask to hide myself. I let my inner self shine through. "As within--so without."

I live my spiritual life by quiet example and not by flaunting my inner growth. I practice what I preach, and my "preaching" comes from the expression of my daily life.

I am thankful for what I have and the person I have become. I no longer compare myself to others nor covet their possessions. I am content with the value of my life just as it is.

Sometimes the addictive urge to overdo is overpowering. When my life becomes unmanageable, I turn control over to my higher power, let go, and accept the peace and tranquility that follows.

I am a complete, independent human being. I do not depend, neither physically nor emotionally, on others for my inner support or happiness.

I know I can count on change, and that security in the material world is an illusion. Therefore, I accept change as an opportunity for spiritual growth, and I openly welcome it.

Today I think about my actions and their consequences before I act on them. If I have any feeling that the consequences could be adverse, I will put off the action for a while and rely on my higher power to tell me what to do.

Today I know the fallacy in trying to rescue another person from the pain of life. I know that if I spend my time saving others, I won't have the time to save myself. I must love and take care of myself first in order to survive.

I will have more fun today because I know that being too serious is not healthy. The child inside of me deserves to be nurtured through humor and play.

I give thanks for my loved ones who have supported me in the past. I readily ask their forgiveness of my past actions and any hurt I have caused them. I become more communicative and closer to them daily.

I realize I am only responsible for my own life. I know that to control others by assuming their responsibilities is an exercise in futility. I decline to try to rob others of their spiritual growth by using their problems to fix mine.

I understand that my tongue can be a sharp sword. Rather than use it for destruction, I choose to use my words to comfort and heal.

I view life's disappointments as opportunities for growth. I choose to learn from them and use them for spiritual advancement. I turn every negative experience into a positive one, viewing these experiences with hope and optimism.

I have inner peace, contentment, and happiness today. I look within myself for fulfillment because I understand that no other person can make me complete.

I face each day with faith and rely on God within me for my direction and purpose. I know my every thought, backed by belief, is an answered prayer.

I realize I cannot change others. The only thing I can change is my thoughts. Therefore, I will continually try to keep the best possible thoughts on my mind.

I know thinking negative thoughts can be a self-fulfilling prophecy, blocking the development of spirituality. I therefore reject feelings of failure, insecurity, inadequacy, and rejection. I cast them aside.

I look within for my spiritual strength which comes one day at a time through prayer, meditation, and living my 12 step program.

I live my life fully, day by day, so that if there is no tomorrow I will feel satisfied that I would not have changed a single thing.

I live my life to please myself, for I know that trying to please everyone else only leads to frustration, disappointment, and lowered self-esteem. Only if I love myself and care for myself first, can I be in a position to love and care for others.

I forgive myself for my imperfections knowing that no one, save Jesus Christ, was perfect. I like myself despite any defects I may possess.

Today I will not yield to the compulsion to overwork. I will work only for the joy and fulfillment that my work contains. When my work becomes unsatisfying, I will put it aside.

Today I will live my life so that I do not manufacture artificial crises by trying to accomplish more than I can. I will be satisfied to achieve a reasonable goal, because I look after myself and my health first.

I feel gratified with my achievements today and will not put myself down for the things I did not get accomplished. I accept my shortcomings today because I look forward to the challenge of tomorrow.

I accept my new being and give thanks for it today, knowing that recovery is a continuing process, and the manifestations will not appear on my time schedule, but when God is ready, I am ready, and the world is ready.

My job is only one aspect of my life. I seek balance between my work and interaction with my family and friends. By maintaining a healthy balance in my life, I insure harmony and peace.

I delegate tasks to others when I can not do them myself. Then I give up control over completion or the manner in which they are accomplished.

Out of my lowest moment, my greatest pain, I start my recovery by accepting my situation and by yielding to God. I have the faith that God will lead me out of hopelessness and despair to happiness, contentment, and ultimate health.

While I sleep tonight, my subconscious mind contemplates, that in truth, I forgive everyone that has ever hurt me.

I reject my illness, for I now realize my every need will be satisfied not through illness, but through health.

I am preparing for a demonstration of spiritual healing. Whether my healing occurs today, or later, I know it is inevitable.

Every illness has been miraculously cured at sometime and at someplace. If it has happened to anyone, it can happen to me.

Tonight I sleep in infinite calm and peace. My thoughts and dreams are only of good and worthwhile concepts.

There is no justification for negative emotions, therefore, I throw out these feelings as soon as I am aware of them. They can no longer influence my life.

From this day forward, I release the guilt of the past. The person I was then is not the person I am now. I live my life now seeking the best in every situation that confronts me.

Today I eat to live and only when I am hungry. Food is no longer a "fix" for feelings of low self-esteem. I now feel good about myself and the health that I deserve. I can now see my new form and figure and give thanks for it in advance.

I feel healthier and happier everyday as I journey down the road to recovery. I realize that the speed I walk is not nearly as important as the fact that I do not stop walking.

Today I am ready and willing to make amends to every person I have harmed. With humility and concern, I advance in my spiritual growth and recovery.

Today I open my mind to God's will and direction by meditation and prayer. I release all my tensions and thoughts of the outside world around me so I can await direction and plan.

The past is already gone and the future never arrives, so I live in the now, knowing that is all I really have.

Today I look for humor and fun in life. I refuse to take myself or the situation I find myself in too seriously. I find relief from stress through the magic of laughter.

I take a gentle approach knowing that nothing of significance is obtained by force. I walk slowly and talk softly so that others will watch my actions and hear what I have to say.

I readily accept disappointments when things in life don't seem to go the way that I want. I turn my will over to God, I expect nothing more than what He wants to provide and when He wants to provide it.

Often softness speaks louder and carries more weight then a loud response. I therefore speak softly and choose my words carefully, so that others will listen and understand what I am saying.

When I think how hard it is and how much effort it takes to effect a change in me, I realize how futile it is to think that I can change others. I therefore give up on trying to change or control those around me and spend my time improving myself.

It is extremely difficult to distinguish between what I am responsible for and what I am not responsible for in life. I am comforted by inner peace and serenity after allowing my higher power to provide advice and direction.

Neither people, material things, nor my addictions can fill an inner emptiness or spiritual void. Therefore, I seek a spiritual path to relieve the emptiness that I feel, and to heal my soul.

I release the unhealthy feelings of guilt and replace them with self-love. I acquit myself of a verdict of guilt because I know it is self-defeating and self-destructive. I forgive myself for any mistakes made in the past and eliminate them from my thoughts and my mind.

I understand that tunnel vision and narrow mindedness keeps one self-centered and retards spiritual growth. Therefore, starting today, I vow to be open minded and tolerant of other's feelings and opinions.

I am a worthwhile, loving, and caring person.

I love myself and like the person I have become.

I project honesty and compassion, and it comes from my soul.

I am valuable to myself, my friends, and to society in general.

I am healthy. My body, mind, and soul have been healed.

I accept the things I cannot change. I possess the courage to change the things I can. God grants me the wisdom to know the difference.

I feel gratitude each day just to be alive and to be able to serve my fellow man.

I am content, fulfilled, and at peace with the world.

I reject destructive thoughts of anger, self-pity, resentment, revenge, jealousy, fear, hate, and continuing guilt or shame. These negative emotions are no longer part of me.

I have a high energy level and am able to achieve everything that is my destiny to achieve today.

My supra-conscious mind is unlimited. Each day I allow it to grow and develop.

I give thanks for the physical, mental, and spiritual healing that has already taken place within me.

I am patient. I know that when I am ready, God is ready, and the world is ready, my goals will become reality.

I cast off the burdens of the past and the anxieties of the future. I live in the present, one day at a time.

My soul is honest, my mind is open, and my entire being is willing to learn.

I will become more spiritual day by day, hour by hour, and minute by minute until my life is in proper balance. I will work the twelve step program, accept it fully, and make it part of me.

I will daily find new ways to strengthen and solidify relationships with my wife, my children, and my parents. I will resist every urge to control their behavior or to change the people they are.

I will conduct my financial affairs and responsibilities in a fair, forthright, and positive manner. I will live within my means and will only desire those things that I need and that I can afford.

I will spend my day living life with all of the enthusiasm I can muster. I will have fun and enjoy life.

I will invest my time, effort, and energy in building up my inner human values instead of material possessions and treasures because material things are only temporary and have no real lasting value.

I look for the humorous aspects of life. I don't take my life too seriously and even laugh at myself from time to time.

I do not worry about the past or the future. I live in the now, and keep moving along my spiritual path. This provides me with serenity and peace.

My friendships are a reflection of who I am inside. As I make significant spiritual growth, some old friends must be replaced with new ones. This makes for a healthier way of living and a better state of mind.

As I share intimacy, I open myself up but do not become a doormat. I drop my barricades but maintain my boundaries. I share myself but retain my individuality and self-respect.

My spiritual path leads me to tranquility at all costs. I evade chaos and conflict, and I avoid controversy and dissension.

I no longer view the opportunity for solitude as an invitation to loneliness. I now relish the time I have for meditation, reflection, and spiritual growth.

Since my future is shaped by my past I will be ever mindful of my history so as to grow and not repeat my errors and mistakes.

I understand that facing life's challenges means taking risks. To continue my recovery I now accept these risks because I know that without feelings life would not be worth living.

I have the courage today to speak out and defend the truth. God grants me the serenity to accept things I cannot change, and courage to change things I can. Today others see the truth in me in every action, thought, and deed.

I am happy today because I accept what is. I know that I need only what is in me to be fulfilled. I do not need external people and possessions to be happy.

I am a dependable, responsible, and trustworthy person who strives for consistency in thought, action, and deed. I make promises only when I believe I can keep them.

Today I will be serene and at peace with myself. I understand it is futile to worry. My time is better spent in active pursuits of my goals in life and on things that can be accomplished.

God grants me the ability to make choices in spite of restrictions, confinements, and indignities. I still exercise my right to think and feel as I please. This mental freedom gives me tranquility and peace of mind.

Today I let go. Obsessive compulsions to control others in the world, which were a part of me yesterday, are no longer part of me today. By yielding this control need to God I now have order, peace, and tranquility in my life.

I continue today down a spiritual path. I will not substitute unhealthy rescues and care-taking relationships for the recovery that spiritual growth provides.

I am a success. I welcome all the good things of life and all the riches of the universe and accept them as I am meant to have them. I rely on God to provide for all of my needs.

Today I will detach myself from unhealthy co-dependent relationships. I know that only by detaching can I continue my spiritual growth and help myself. I make this hard choice out of love and compassion.

I will take my inventory again today. I honestly look at my good points and my defects. Regardless of what my inventory shows I will continue to love myself as a valuable human being.

Today I will search for the best in every situation. I prefer to see my glass as half full instead of half empty. I have a choice in how I view the world and I choose to view it with optimism, enthusiasm, and hope.

I confess to God my inability to control life around me. My addictive needs have made my life unmanageable. By turning over my will to Him, my spiritual recovery is guaranteed.

Today I freely and openly admit when I am wrong or make a mistake. I approach life with humility, for I know it is not humanly possible to always be right.

Today I take care of and look after myself. I will not allow guilt, "should haves", rescues, and the need to please others to cause me to drown in a sea of codependency.

Even though today I take care of myself first, I will not become so self-centered as to neglect others. I will always make the time to love and care for others, but now I express that concern in healthy ways.

When faced with difficult times, such as now, I will not sit back and wait for life to correct itself. I will, starting now, take positive steps to correct the problem. My inspiration and direction flow from God and He certainly has the ability to bring harmony back into my life.

I now readily admit that my life has become unmanageable due to trying to acquire power, success, and wealth. Today I turn my life over to God to manage it for me, realizing that by doing so I will receive all of the abundances in life that I need and deserve.

I will start today trusting more in my fellow human beings. Trust is a treasured emotion springing from hope and faith. I know that fear is the greatest roadblock to the development of trust, therefore, I ask God to calm my anxieties and give me peace of mind.

I feel complete and content even when alone. I do not need another person constantly by my side to feel good. My feelings of contentment come from within and not from the external world and other people.

Today is the first day of the rest of my life. I will ask God to grant me the serenity to accept the things I cannot change, courage to change the things I can, and the wisdom to know the difference.

I will from this day forward be true to myself and stop trying to pease everyone else. I respect myself and my opinions and do not change them lightly just to please others.

I will take time and make time for prayer and meditation. I will silently wait for answers to come. In humility I will ask for strength and guidance from God knowing that my prayers are always answered. When I feel afraid, vulnerable, dependent, and alone, I let go and let God. He takes control and everything becomes right again.

Although I don't always know why things happen, I do believe everything happens for a reason. God knows that reason and allows me to function through acceptance and faith.

When I strive for spiritualization, I do so to achieve a balance in life and to decrease my destructive, addictive habits. I do not give up my contact and interaction with the physical world however, because the key to recovery lies in the balance between the physical and the spiritual.

Starting today, I will see things from others' points of view. By limiting my ego and showing compassion, I will become more understanding and sensitive to the needs of others.

Today I release my feelings of resentment, anger, and hate. As I give these feelings up, l feel love and contentment with my life and a closeness to my higher power. The release of these negative emotions allows my body to heal.

I await a message from God to show me how to help others. When that message arrives, I will act on it directly with enthusiasm, trust, and faith.

I change from day to day and therefore require constant re-evaluation. My recovery is a never ending process where I learn to understand and love myself first, so that thereafter I can love and understand others.

Today I will bring duty, obligation, and work into perspective. My job and the company no longer is my primary focus. Now I achieve a balance between my work, my family, and other associations.

Beginning today, I will be truthful and honest with myself and others. No longer will I allow "white lies," half-truths, or other dishonesty to be part of my thinking. I will take comfort in the fact that consistency in my thoughts, actions, and deeds will lead to peace and harmony of my soul.

I give up worry of all the negative fearful things in my life. Most of them I can't control anyway. The anxiety that I felt for so long is no longer a part of me. I release my nervousness to God who is ready to accept it.

Today life is exciting for me as I continue on my spiritual treasure hunt. God directs my journey and provides me peace of mind.

I surround myself with people who have similar values and ideals to mine, people who help me grow spiritually, and fulfill my potential.

I give freely today to those in need. I give anonymously when appropriate, and without selfish expectations of wanting anything in return.

I do not put off until tomorrow the essentials that have to be dealt with today. When I complete a task I cross it off of my list and this action makes me feel more content and hopeful for the rest of my day.

I spend today finding or continuing a relationship with one other person who understands me and cares about me. During difficult times I use this person as a sounding board and trust him or her with my emotions and feelings.

When I have feelings that the grass is greener in another place, I remember that only spiritual changes make any significant difference. Therefore I do not look to changes in the external environment, but to my higher power to improve the quality of my life.

Today I will acknowledge my successes and admit my shortcomings. I reject false pride and replace it with humility. I will not allow fears of rejection to limit my truth and honesty.

Today I release my resentments one by one. Holding on to these bad feelings harms me and keeps me from healing. When I forgive and fill my mind with love, resentments just melt away.

Today I put all of my troubles, worries, and anxieties in the hands of God and leave them there. I put my thoughts and efforts into things where I can affect some change.

I will do one thing spontaneously today. I reject the limits of my daily routine and the confines of my habits.

Today I project my true feelings to the world in an honest and forthright manner. I no longer hide behind a mask to prevent others from seeing the true me. Since I claim worthy spiritual characteristics for my life, I am happy for others to experience the real me.

I approach life with a feeling of humility and self-love. I admit both my strengths and my weaknesses. I know inner peace comes from a close relationship to God.

Today I am strong enough to detach myself from the object of my co-dependency. I know "tough love" is necessary for healing in both of us.

I am what 1 think. As more positive thoughts fill up my mind and consciousness, fewer unhealthy destructive ones remain. I repeat my affirmations as often as possible.

Today I admit I am powerless over my addiction and turn my will and the direction of my life over to God. I pray for His direction and open my mind to wait for His answer.

I view life's disappointments as an opportunity for growth. I choose to learn from them and use them for spiritual advancement. I will turn every negative experience into a positive one, and view these experiences with hope and optimism.

I have inner peace, contentment, and happiness today. I look within myself for fulfillment because I understand that no other person can make me complete.

I face each day with faith and courage. I rely on God who lives within me, for direction and purpose. I know my every thought, backed by belief, is an answered prayer.

I replace the word "should" from my vocabulary because it just brings me down. I couldn't "should have" done anything. I leave all actions and shortcomings of the past, in the past. They are no longer part of me.

I know fear to be a negative emotion that can be a self-fulfilling prophecy blocking the development of spirituality. I therefore reject feelings of failure, insecurity, and inadequacy. I cast them aside.

Today I take responsibility for my thoughts, actions, and deeds. I do not blame others for my problems. I release all resentments from my mind because resentments block my spiritual healing.

In the inner vacuum of my soul I reject anger, hate, and resentments so that the space can be refilled with happiness, love, and contentment, and I can continue to travel the spiritual path in life.

I rejoice with feelings of gratitude for all of the things I have and the person I have become. I will no longer complain about the things I want but do not possess, because I know that God will provide for all of my needs.

I love myself first, because only then is it possible to transfer that self-love into helping and caring for someone else. When I help others it is to provide the means for them to help themselves and not to control them or to run their lives.

I realize it takes courage to change my life. I commit the courage necessary to turn over my inability to control my addictions to God and to accept His direction in my life.

I look within for my security. I understand that external forces like my job, my relationships, and my benefactors do not provide lasting security. I am confident in the ability of a higher power to sustain mc and protect me from harm.

As I think quality, spiritual thoughts, I develop a quality, spiritual life. Therefore today I will dwell on thoughts of love, compassion, and brotherly concern with all whom I come in contact.

I feel comfortable with making decisions. Even if my decision later turns out not to be the best, it is better to take some stand than to refuse to decide and become a victim of life.

There are many forks along the spiritual paths down my road of life. Today I choose the path of self-improvement, and I resist the path of self-centeredness, hopelessness, and despair.

Today I realize and fully accept the fact that I am good and valuable just as I am. As much as being successful by the world's terms is desirable, it is even more desirable to not need the worldly trappings of success to feel complete and fulfilled. I am now complete, fulfilled, and whole.

I am a good person. I like myself. I love myself.

I have a radiant glow that surrounds me and comes from within.

I am one with God who resides within me and answers my every prayer.

As I walk through life today, I will do unto others as I would have them do unto me. I will keep this thought foremost and express it in every action and deed.

I take time today for quiet meditation, for it is through opening up receptive times that I am able to receive answers to my prayers.

Even though I now realize that acts and deeds speak louder then words, I will remember not to say things that will contradict my real thoughts and feelings. In this way I will not mislead myself or others.

When I allow even slight dishonesty to decrease my personal integrity, my spiritual growth suffers. Help me God, to be honest with myself and welcome anyone who tells me the truth about me.

I understand that trying to control others is not only self-defeating, but is a measure of my own insecurity. I will, starting today, begin trusting more in a simple act of faith.

When I pray, it's not to change the will of God. My ultimate ambition is to conform my life to God's will in order to have the best that I possibly can.

Whether by a profound miracle or a chilling silence, my prayers will be answered. However, they are not always answered by human preference, but by divine understanding. They are always answered for the best.

Even though I have recently felt tired, ineffective, and depressed, I reject these feelings. I see myself as energetic, happy, and full of enthusiasm for life. I will get up and get going. Through activity I will become productive once again.

Today I sincerely and honestly forgive everyone who has ever hurt me. I do this not so much for them, but for myself. Now I can and do accept forgiveness for every error or mistake I have ever made. I now start anew with no continuing guilt or shame.

I feel sensual. My body tingles with enthusiasm for life.

I will accomplish everything I am destined to do today. There are no limitations to what I can do.

I am dependable and do not put off the things I want to do.

The truth is within me, and I radiate it in all of my dealings.

I reject all destructive thoughts and actions and think only of compassion and love.

I see myself having already reached goals that can not be denied me. I give thanks for the accomplishments now.

Even when I am down, I look up. I look for comfort, love, and understanding. While I am looking up, I'm developing my spiritual values and healing my soul.

Part of God is always with me. God, continues to protect me, guide me, and help me make the right decisions in everything I do.

I care about others. When they speak, I actively listen, pay attention, and really try to understand what they are trying to say.

I remain at peace and secure knowing that what is right and just will ultimately prevail. Therefore I don't allow the initial appearance of injustice to upset my tranquility, harmony, and faith.

God, I know you love me unconditionally, just as I am right now. I radiate your love for me to others all over the world.

When I pray, let me sometimes pray in silence, aware of the divine presence of God within me. I await instruction and direction in these times of silence.

If I worry about the outcome of a particular situation or problem, I will do the worrying before the decision is made. Afterwards, I will relax, and since the wheels have been set in motion, allow them to turn to their conclusion.

I concentrate and work on only one thing at a time. My attention is directed on what I am doing right now. Other things can wait.

Today I will be more friendly and helpful to other people. I will be more tolerant and less critical. I will interpret other's words and actions in the most favorable light.

I count my blessings. I am grateful for another day to fulfill my destiny.

Today, and everyday, I deliver more than I am being paid to deliver.

Whenever I make a mistake, or get knocked down by life, I don't look back at it too long. I shake off my blunders.

I always reward my long hours of labor and toil in the very best way, surrounded by my family.

I build this day on a foundation of pleasant thoughts. I am a creature of God and have the power to achieve any dream by lifting my thoughts.

I let my actions speak for me, but I am forever on my guard against the terrible traps of false pride and conceit that can halt my progress.

Each day is a special gift from God, and while life may not always be fair, I never allow the pains, hurdles, and handicaps of the moment to poison my attitude and my future.

I never again clutter my days and nights with so many menial and unimportant things that I have no time to accept a real challenge when it comes along.

I live this day as though it will be my last.

Beginning today, I treat everyone I meet, friend or foe, loved one or stranger, as if he were going to be dead at midnight.

I laugh at myself and at life.

I never neglect the little things.

I welcome every morning with a smile. I look on the new day as another special gift from my Creator, another golden opportunity to complete what I was unable to finish yesterday.

I will achieve my grand dream, a day at a time, so I set my goals for each day.

I never allow anyone to rain on my parade and thus cast a pail of gloom and defeat on the entire day. Nothing external can have any power over me unless I allow it.

I search for the seed of good in every adversity.

There is no justification for holding on to negative emotions, therefore, I will throw out all those feelings as soon as I am aware of them. They will no longer influence my life.

I live for the truth and am honest with myself I realize it makes little difference who's right, but a lot of difference in what's right.

I know that love is my greatest need.

I am a vital human being with a valid and important purpose here on earth.

I realize that true happiness lies within me. Therefore I go within, so I don't have to go without.

Chapter Eighteen Your New Life

Your willingness to relax and let go has put you into a life transforming mode that will give you the strength you need to overcome the conflicts you encounter in your life. I am not saying it will be easy. You need to formalize your commitment and keep it foremost in your mind. Remember that as a baby after you took your first step, the rest was easy. When you surrender your will and life to God, you find a genuine way to satisfy all your emotional, physical, and spiritual needs. You are restored to wholeness by renouncing the old ways and scaling the barriers that blocked your recovery.

We must continue to take personal inventory so that we stay on course and do not fall prey to the old patterns of denial and the destructive patterns that so easily led us astray while we were feeding our addictions. We make a confident and conscious decision to get on with our lives and share our spiritual awakening with those around us and with the world at large. We celebrate each unfolding experience in our life by sharing our new strength and love with those to whom we come into contact.

Our spiritual transformation helps others find the courage to face their own needs and perhaps serves as a true inspiration for change. This is part of the answer to helping our loved ones. The focus now shifts from doing for oneself to sharing our seeds of wisdom and understanding with others. The life changing potential that we now carry within us must be shared with others if we are to become a partner in the desperately needed shift back to love.

We must be consistent when we acknowledge our dependence on God. God is the source of our success and will always be there as we meditate and look to Him for direction. Though hard at first, it soon becomes easy to relax and lean on God for His understanding, acceptance, and guidance.

If you reach a point later when you lack direction, remember to rework the five steps of your recovery program. The way you respond to difficult situations in life will be influenced by your vigilant adherence to the program's principles.

To embark on the journey of complete recovery means you have to be ever vigilant in your internal message delivery system. Your thoughts must be crystal clear, appropriate, and focused. Never again will you need to rely on your addictive behaviors to meet you needs.

Over time, repetition will make it easier to recognize the minute you start to drift into patterns that are not compatible with your new life. Repetition is necessary not only in the recovery process but also serves as the springboard for the future spiritual stability you wish to maintain. You are now on a path of spiritual awakening that will allow growth, and as you reach each plateau, your communication with God will become a constant source of direction.

You will attain the peace and happiness that you were born to enjoy. When you unlock the door and discover what God wants you to do with your life, your life will become a road map toward the destiny that you are here to fulfill.

As you increase your spiritual understanding, your sense of direction will become clear. Part of this direction includes the responsibility to share your new found wisdom and understanding with others. In so doing you not only strengthen your resolve to seek God's will in your life, but you also make a positive and significant contribution to the world. May you always have the happiness, peace, and love that you deserve. Remember that as a child of God, you are on a spiritual quest to gain understanding and to seek the path back to your Creator. However, while you are on the earth, work diligently to make a contribution, if for no other reason, for the sake of love. We are all children of God, and in that sense all brothers and sisters. Each of us is valuable to the Creator and worthy of being loved. Love is our greatest need.

This book was written to help fulfill God's mission for my life. Initially I asked, then I listened, and finally made a decision to yield my will to His. This is my attempt to share the spiritual understanding and awakening which has so dramatically changed my life. By sharing this understanding, I am fulfilling my destiny, and feel both privileged and blessed to feel the Divine presence and power of God surrounding me working in the world. Hopefully this material will have a significant impact in your life as you search to understand and fulfill your destiny. May God guide and richly bless your endeavors. Remember to relax and start enjoying the beautiful melody of peace and love as your divine purpose unfolds.

Now share your wisdom and understanding with those who lack your spiritual understanding. As you continue to search for and follow the principles you have learned, love and happiness will always be with you. Welcome to your new life!

Epilogue

I tell everyone that one of the requirements for this program to be 100% effective is to truly believe that it will work. When you go to see a medical doctor to cure your pneumonia and he gives you penicillin, it doesn't make much difference if you believe it is the right drug to cure you. If it is, it will. If it is not, it won't. Likewise, if you visit a surgeon for a hernia repair, it doesn't make much difference whether or not you believe in the surgeon's ability to cure you with an operation. Either he has the skill to affect the cure or he doesn't.

Addiction, however, is a spiritual disease, and spiritual cures are totally dependent on faith or belief. If you do not believe that the treatment will work, you will not follow the discipline of the program. And of course, if you do not continue the treatment it will fail. Curing this disease is not as easy as taking a pill for 10 days and it is more time consuming than a surgical operation.

Perhaps the most difficult task you will be asked to do is to discipline your thoughts and actions. Yet this is the only way to get a permanent, total cure from the problem.

Not everybody who has read this book will agree with its concepts. Some will reject the premise that addiction is a spiritual disease that requires a spiritual cure. Some will not continue treatment for one reason or another. Both groups will fail to cure their addictive disease process.

A few will read this book, believe in the ideas, and fully act on that belief. For those lucky individuals, their disease will be cured totally and permanently. They cannot fail! I sincerely hope you are among those fortunate individuals. If you are not ready for treatment yet, don't throw this book away. Just put it back on your library shelf to wait for the day you "hit bottom." Addiction results in all sorts of bad things happening and eventually in death. Until that day comes, the answer will be waiting.

Contact information:

Rev. Winn Henderson, MD

www.freedomfromaddiction4.com
freedomfromaddiction.libsyn.com

828-508-7981

Endorsements

What other authors have said about The Four Questions (which is a previous edition of Freedom From Addiction 4 with no significant changes between the two editions).

If you read one self help book in the next year, let it be "The Four Questions." It takes over your mind, reads itself to you, and changes your perspective on life. If your life is not what you want it to be this is the best investment you could ever make to improve it. Dr. Henderson articulates the warmest, friendliest, and most precise path to personal happiness that you could ever find in print." Dr. Jay Lehr, Author of Fit, Firm, and 50.

The Four Questions reads well and is easy to follow...it delves deep into the psychologic. His questions are spiritual and psychological in nature and get inside to break up fallow ground and then to exorcise the demons within. Jim Price, Newspaper columnist, Midsummer Night's Dream.

"I loved, loved, loved reading Dr. Henderson's new book, The Four Questions. It is the book on addiction (of every kind and nature). This book should be used as a text book and made a must reading in every high school and college throughout the world to make this earth a better place to live in.

If you, or a family member or friend, wants to effectively and inexpensively (just the cost of the book) get rid of any type of addiction or addictive behavior that adversely affects your happiness and joy of living, this book is a must." Sidney Freeman, Member of the New York and Florida Bar. Author of Life After Death.

"You haven't missed a thing, in terms of naming the deadening effects of addiction and also setting out a straight forward plan for exactly what needs to be done about it. There is not a person in the United States who couldn't benefit from your insights." Christiane Northrup, M.D; Author of Women's Bodies, Women's Wisdom.

"Dr. Henderson's Book, The Four Questions, challenges us to face the reality of our lives. Your answers to his vital questions could alter your life forever. This is a life changing book that can make the world a better place for all who read it." Lester Sauvage, M.D; Pioneer Coronary Bypass Heart Surgeon and Author of The Open Heart: Secret To Happiness, You Can Beat heart Disease: Prevention and Treatment, and The Better Life Diet: A Simple Plan For A Long and Youthful Life.

I believe your book will be a real contribution to the world." Jed Diamond, Author of The Warrior's Journey Home: Healing Men, Healing the Planet, and Looking For Love In All The Wrong Places: Overcoming Romantic and Sexual Addictions.

"Life is too short and important to waste your precious time in pain and suffering. The Four Questions will lift your spirits and help you create the life you desire and deserve." Dr. Ellen Kreidman, Author of the New York Times bestsellers: Light His Fire and Light Her Fire and more recently Is There Sex After Kids? The Ten Second Kiss, and Single No More. Developer of a highly successful relationship infomercial. keynote speaker, seminar developer and facilitator. and on-line relationship advise expert.

"...your sincerity and genuiness shine through. I love your attempt to reach out and help others. You put your heart and soul in this and my prayers are with you." Shelly Marshall, Professional Speaker and Author of Day by Day, Young, Sober and Free, and Your Dream of Recovery.

"The Four Questions touches at the very essence of life. It guides the way to healing, recovery, and fullness of life at the deepest levels." Brenda Shoshanna PhD. Psychologist and Psychotherapist. Author of 365 Ways to Give Thanks.

"I learned a great deal from your book, The Four Questions. I believe learning from each other is what life is all about." Dr. Anneliese Widman. Author of My Female, My Male, My Self and God, A Modern Woman in Search of Her Soul, Ascending to Reunion, and Rage at God.

"Dr. Henderson has an infectious energy, sincerity, and commitment that leaps out at you from every page. Reading this short, clear book gives you both the motivation and the method to get that monkey off your back." Dr. J.Robert Adams, Author of Surviving Death and NIH researcher.

"The Four Questions" is filled to the brim and overflowing with solid, helpful, practical, enlightening, positive ideas for everyone who is addicted Well done, Dr. Henderson, very well done!" Dottie Walters, CSP, Author of Speak and Grow Rich, President of Walters international Speakers Bureau. Publisher of Sharing Ideas.

"What if you had a million dollar inheritance and nobody told you? The Four Questions is a great guide for finding your inheritance. It provides

a practical tool for shifting into high gear.....more giving, more happiness, more of the abundance that is our birthright." Bonnie St. John Deane, Olympic Silver Medal Winner, Rhode's Scholar, Author of Succeeding Sane.

"Dr. Henderson's The Four Questions is a practical, accessible, straight-talking guide to overcoming addictions. It advocates that people do so by nurturing their spiritual resources, thereby opening up new hope, pride, opportunities, and sources of meaning in life.

It speaks most strongly to people who embrace Christian beliefs and values, whether or not they adhere to any particular denomination. The author's earnest desire to motivate and help people relieve suffering and find greater happiness shine clearly through the pages of the book, as does the sense that he 'walks' his own talk." Mary Jacobsen, M.S.W., PhD, a licensed psychotherapist and social worker, teacher, counselor, career coach and workshop leader. She is the author of Hand Me Down Dreams: How Families Influence Our Career Paths and How We Can Reclaim Them.

"I loved The Four Questions! You can't get any simpler than this and end up on top. Cheers to Dr. Henderson for making us look within for our own answers. Micki Voisard, author of Cancer, Then Healing.

"We long for fulfillment in our lives and in ignorance seek ways to fill that longing with many addictive behaviors. Dr. Henderson, in his book, The Four Questions, guides the reader in awakening to the source of wholeness and fulfillment that resides within each of us, which is the most important discovery we will ever make as spiritual beings living a human experience. A must read for everyone. "Joyce Nelson Patenaude, PhD; a licensed psychologist and author of Too Tired To Keep Running, Too Scared To Stop and Change Your Beliefs, Change Your Life.

"Dr. Henderson gets to the basics when he asks "the four questions." He gives the reader the enlightenment to answer the questions and a blueprint for living a successful life. Read his book and learn how to be a free and complete person." Barbara Del Buono, author of Acknowledged A Man, victim's rights and brain injury advocate.

"The Four Questions" is an important book with a lot of down-to-earth wisdom. I believe that Dr. Henderson's advice can be of great help and encouragement to people who are fearful and hurting. He covers many aspects of human need: depression, addictions, and the often unfulfilled search for meaning and happiness in life." Cristoph Arnold, Founder of Bruderhof, Minister, Peace advocate, Editor of The Plough, and author of several books including: A Plea For Purity, A Little Child Shall Lead Them, I Tell You a Mystery, Seventy Time Seven, and Cries From The Heart.

"If you ask yourself trivial questions, your life will seem a soap opera. If you ask yourself great questions, your life will be a life of greatness. This book, about these four great questions of the ages, will help you step out of a quiet life of desperation and move forward into a powerful life of inspiration, a life of significance and meaning." Dr. Richard Bellamy, Author of 12 Secrets for Manifesting Your Vision. Inspiration, and Purpose: How to Make Your Dreams Come True.

"The Four Questions is curatively profound." Dr. Larry Clifton, Author of Your Platform is the World.

"In terms of spiritual understanding, The Four Questions, hits the mark....a bulls eye! It explains simply four of the most complex

questions man has ever contemplated." Gordon A. "Stumpy" Harris. Attorney, Seminar Leader, Author of The Mind-Body-Son method For Weight Reduction

"The Four Questions contains a wealth of knowledge on the four crucial questions which lead to inner peace, happiness, and hope. Dr. Henderson replaces ignorance, not with bliss, but with adequate information on addictions and the human struggle." Reverend Sharon Colbert- Author of Stand With Angels: Conversations With God.

"Addiction is the black plague of the 20th century. Dr. Henderson's book, The Four Questions, gives those who are ready a concrete, step by step way to become whole and truly free. Dr. Karen PurcelI. Naturopathic Physician, Clinical Nutritionist, Professional Speaker, Founder of the WINS Foundation, and Author of Simplified Nutritional Handbook.

"Doctor Henderson's book, The Four Questions, can easily help everyone find his or her mission in life. Bill Staton, CFA, CPA, America's Money Coach, and Author of 60-Minute Investing and Lifetime Riches- The Seven Secrets to Multiplying Your Wealth.

"The Four Questions, provides all the answers to health, wealth, and happiness." Dr. Eric Kaplan, Author of Lifestyles of the Fit and Famous and Awaken the Wellness Within.

www.ingramcontent.com/pod-product-compliance
Lightning Source LLC
Chambersburg PA
CBHW040854120626
46551CB00001B/8